Secrets of the Soul

Jill M. Jackson

DEDICATION

My heart is full as I think of everyone who helped me birth this book.

To my husband Daniel. Thank you for working hard every day allowing me to realize my dreams. I look forward to the magic we will continue to create together. I love you more than I ever knew it was possible to love.

To my dad, Buddy, thank you for being my biggest cheerleader. No matter how many times my journey has changed course, you are right by my side offering any support you can. I am so blessed to have chosen a father who is also a mentor and friend. I love you so much.

To my beautiful mom, Gail. You were my greatest teacher with the Law of Polarity. I never knew the depths of deep grief until you stepped into the Other World. Through learning how to live again, you taught me how to love even more. Thank you for being my Angel, my mom, and my friend.

To my sister Wendy. I'm so happy it was you walking this crazy road with me from so long ago. Thank you for being my voice of reason when I need it. We are beyond lucky that we that we can call each other sister and friend. I love you more.

To my editor, Jo Ann Langseth. I am forever grateful to the Universe for putting you in my path. You are truly an editor extraordinaire. This book would not be what it is without your remarkable editing genius.

To William Kelly, who designed the book cover, thank you. You hit a home run with my first book and took us straight to the winner's circle with this one. Your intuitive skills in design are truly mind blowing.

Thank you to all my spiritual teachers and mentors who helped guide my way, graciously sharing your knowledge with me.

And last but certainly not least, thank you to my Spirit Team, who always has my back. Thankfully, you have been able to retire the etheric two by four, as I have learned to listen to your guidance, even in the most subtle ways. I honor and appreciate each of you.

Table of Contents

Chapter 1   My Secret Story
Chapter 2   Spiritual Secrets
Chapter 3   Law of Attraction and The Secret
Chapter 4   Spiritual Universal Laws
Chapter 5   Past Lives, Soul Contracts, & Soul Tribes
Chapter 6   Life Path and Purpose
Chapter 7   Frequency and Manifestation Magic
Chapter 8   Collective Wisdom
Chapter 9   Painting Your Masterpiece

Introduction

To those of you who read *The Secret* and fell in love with its life-changing concepts, this book is for you! Throughout the past decade, awareness and consciousness expansion has seen explosive growth, and now is the perfect time to delve deeper into the thoughts and ponderings about the true meaning of why we are here and what we came here to accomplish.

To those of you who read *The Secret* and identified with its fundamental concepts yet felt there were deeper treasures yet to unearth, this book is for you, too!

Or might there be areas in your life where you applied the principles taught in *The Secret* but were not successful in manifesting those particular hopes and dreams?

As someone who has always considered herself a powerful manifestor, I fell in love with The Law of Attraction and *The Secret* many years ago. I was excited to ride the wave of exhilaration over the energy created by the success of the book and the movie. However, as you will see in Chapter One, I stumbled and fell in a significant area of my life in which I was unable to manifest what I wanted more than anything at the time. I fell into the depths of depression, not only from my inability to achieve what I wanted so badly, but also for feeling defeated in a type of "manifestation failure" that made me feel even worse.

After a period of grieving and mourning, I decided to go on a quest to find answers to my failure at manifesting. Over the years, as the answers came flooding in, it occurred to me that many others must surely be experiencing this as well. When my clients started talking about their own "failures" and seeking answers from a deep soul level as to why they had not succeeded, I then made the commitment to write this book and share the wisdom I had acquired throughout my own journey.

What I learned along the way and what I will share with you is that while the Law of Attraction is quite powerful, there are many other spiritual laws at our disposal that work hand in hand with the Law of Attraction. Soul contracts, past lives, and karma play a major role in this arena as well.

As I often enjoy doing in other areas of my life, I decided to step outside the box, so to speak, regarding the composition of this book. My Spirit Team encouraged me to write a fictional story to complement the book's nonfictional concepts. And for the proverbial cherry on top, my amazing husband Daniel received the inspiration that the first part of the story should serve as the prologue. and the final part of the fictional short story should be the epilogue. I sincerely hope you enjoy these fictive bookends which use real-life examples to further underscore the concepts explained in the book.

In closing, I encourage you to purchase a journal specifically as a companion to this book. At the close of the chapters, I suggest that you journal about how the ideas pertain to areas and situations in your own life. After all, my goal in opening up painful chapters of my own life regarding my personal grief at so-called manifestation failure is to help others with similar challenges, not only to transcend them, but to transmute the seeming negative into something positive and powerful. In this wild and wonderful human experience, one of our greatest lessons is learning to honor our grief and seeming setbacks by transmuting them into something even more profound.

Through deep revelations and understandings, we are provided beautiful gifts to evolve. It is my sincere prayer that this book is one of those gifts for you.

Infinite Blessings!

Prologue

The alarm clock blasted its deafening buzz way too early as far as Mandy was concerned. One of her New Year's resolutions was to stop hitting the snooze button multiple times, so she forced herself out of bed to face the day. The strong aroma of French roast coffee brewing helped ease some of her disappointment that it was only Thursday. As Mandy enjoyed her coffee, she reflected on the exciting seminar she had attended the weekend before. The words of the speaker echoed in her mind as she replayed the message. The speaker was a Law of Attraction expert and her promise to everyone in attendance was that they could manifest anything their hearts desired.

Still charged with adrenaline from the energy of the weekend, Mandy had come to the bold conclusion that she was going to take charge of her life and begin manifesting all her dreams. As she walked to the other room to grab her journal, she congratulated herself on getting out of bed without hitting the snooze button, giving herself more time to reflect on all the things she was going to manifest using the Law of Attraction. Her cat Theodore followed, loudly meowing that it was time for his breakfast. "Give me a moment, Teddy. I'm going for my journal while my inspiration is still bubbling!"

Mandy made a mental note to take her journal to work with her so she could write down some dreams while she was eating her salad at lunch. "The first thing I will write," she confided to the seemingly disinterested feline, "is how John's proposal will unfold. I'm sure it will happen next month, on Valentine's Day!" Licking his paws after a delicious breakfast, Teddy reflected on a dream of his own. *I wish Mom would go ahead and schedule that appointment with the animal communicator. That way, I can relay the message that I despise John. Why can't Mom see he is selfish and self-centered and can barely tolerate the fact that I'm still here with her? I, her faithful companion! The nerve of him! Surely there is a kind-hearted man out there who will shower her with love and give me the proper ear rubs that I deserve!*

As Mandy bundled up, preparing to face the brutally cold Michigan morning, she gave Theodore a big hug and kiss goodbye. "Make yourself useful today while I'm at work," she joked. As she drove to work, she ruminated on how she was going to manifest a job promotion. After all, she deserved this promotion. She had been with the company for five years, was never late, and always kept a positive attitude. *No, this is not my dream job,* Mandy admitted to herself, *but it pays well, and I get two weeks' vacation every year.*

Since Sunday, Mandy had been writing her name with the title supervisor after it. The speaker at the Law of Attraction seminar taught that if you write things down, the energy becomes stronger, and it's more likely that you will manifest what you desire.

As Mandy walked through the office plaza where she spent the majority of her waking hours, she felt a slight pang of frustration as Rebecca stopped her at the coffee station to gossip about the new cute guy in accounting. Mandy was far more interested in getting her desk organized, excited to celebrate the promotion that she just knew was coming any day now. Plus, Mandy thought to herself, *I'm committed to John and I'm looking forward to marrying him and starting a family*. Her own doubts along with her sister's warnings about John tried to force themselves into the corridors of her mind, but Mandy was quick to dismiss those negative thoughts. She loved John and just knew he would eventually come around to enjoy with her the things that made her heart soar. Rescuing animals and spending time on sunny sandy beaches were high on her wish list. But John was a workaholic who never made time to take her to the Florida beaches, despite her asking him countless times. *Maybe, I can manifest a beach trip for us*, Mandy thought hopefully. Smiling politely at Rebecca, she grabbed her coffee and headed to her desk. As she settled in to begin her monotonous duties, the phone at her desk rang. Tim, the human resources manager, was on the line and asked her to come see him. Mandy almost skipped to his office as she knew her promotion was about to be offered. *Wow, this Law of Attraction stuff works quickly!* she jubilated.

"Good morning, Tim," Mandy chirped as she sat down by his desk. "I hope you enjoyed your vacation." Tim nodded nervously, moving quickly on to the business at hand. "Mandy, you have been with our company for five years now, and we truly appreciate your service and loyalty to our firm." Mandy took a deep breath, anticipating the excitement of the job promotion announcement she was about to receive. Tim paused. "However, our shareholders approved a larger year-end bonus than normal for the President and Chairman, so we are forced to make some adjustments to accommodate the budget. I'm terribly sorry, but we are going to be eliminating your position," Mandy shook her head in disbelief. This was not possible. "I don't understand," she said. "What am I supposed to do?" She continued, "Is there any severance or compensation for my years of service?" Tim smiled proudly as he explained to her that he had been able to secure two weeks' severance for her. Feeling as if she might pass out at any moment, Mandy blurted, "Two weeks? Are you kidding me? After five years of loyal service and never missing any days other than my vacation? This is what my loyalty and hard work is worth to this firm?" Eager to end the unpleasant exchange so he could devour his donut waiting patiently behind him, Tim pushed the paper toward Mandy for her to sign.

Mandy fought back her tears as she cleaned out the desk that had been home to her for so many seemingly never-ending days over the years. As she drove home, allowing the sadness to envelop her in waves of sobbing and despair, Mandy screamed out to no one in particular, "Why was I not able to manifest this promotion? I did everything instructed at the workshop!" Thankfully, she'd at least have the faithful Teddy awaiting her return. Petting his velvety orange and gray hair always calmed her down.

Immediately upon walking into the house, Mandy put down her boxed desk materials and called John. In her message she told him she really needed to talk to him. Washing the streaked makeup from her face, she decided to wait until Monday to start looking for another job. After all, maybe John would end up proposing early, she mused. This thought brought a smile to her tear-stained face. Manifestation revisions would have to start right away! She would stay calm, prepare a cup of Earl Grey tea, and work on her Law of Attraction journal to manifest the proposal. For good measure, she decided to go ahead and visualize the gorgeous home they would live in together. For a brief moment, the voice in her head reminded her that she and John had very different visions as to what their dream home would be. John wanted a condo in the city close to his office, while Mandy wanted a single-family home with a large yard for all the animals she would rescue to frolic in. *I'm sure if I visualize strongly enough, John will come around to seeing how special a house with a large yard will be.* Mandy begin cutting out houses and photos of wedding gowns from the countless magazines she'd collected. As she looked out at the bleak midwinter day, Mandy continued to wonder what she had done wrong in manifesting her job promotion. *I will need to put more effort into the other things I manifest,* she vowed. She also allowed herself to dream of sunny bright days at the beach, and felt a fresh wave of disappointment that John did not enjoy the beach. She shook her head, wondering how on earth she was still living in Michigan when there was no one she knew who disliked the snow and cold as much as she. *Oh, well, at least with my new tools from the seminar I'll be able to manifest beach trips after I'm married to John,* Mandy reassured herself.

After enjoying the last sip of her tea, Mandy decided to go look for the business card of that psychic her friend Denise had told her about. Denise had raved about the psychic's accuracy and life-changing revelations. Maybe it was time to give her a try. When she had mentioned it to John in the past, he had laughed, telling her not to waste her time and money on such nonsense. Thinking about this reminded her that John had not called her back. She told herself he was probably stuck in meetings and would call later. They had a date planned for Friday evening, but Mandy decided she would tell him about her job loss on the phone. As if on cue, Teddy jumped up on the desk and landed on the psychic's card. A clear sign! She would dial the number. What harm could it possibly do? Miss Thelma answered the phone on the third ring and told Mandy that fate must have intervened because she just had a cancellation come up for that afternoon. "Can you be here at 3:00?" Miss Thelma asked. Nervously, Mandy told her she would be there.

As Mandy pulled into the driveway of the small house, she was not sure what to expect. What she found on the other side of the door when Ms. Thelma opened it was the farthest thing from what she had imagined. Ms. Thelma was short and old. As her bony fingers reached out to shake Mandy's hand, Mandy felt a chill run down her back. What could that sensation be all about? Never before had she been in someone's presence who made her feel so very calm yet energetic at the same time. This sensation was foreign and confusing to Mandy, yet she dutifully followed Ms. Thelma into her reading room. Mandy looked around the room in childlike delight. There were shiny crystals everywhere. When she was a small child, Mandy had had a special affinity for rocks and crystals. The pleasant scent of sandalwood and frankincense curled and danced through the air from Ms. Thelma's dragon-shaped incense burner. Ms. Thelma introduced Mandy to the gorgeous black cat sitting at her feet.

"This is Magic, my protector," Ms. Thelma explained. "We have traveled together through many incarnations." Mandy was not quite sure she believed in reincarnation but decided to remain open. She quickly concluded that she was not going to share this experience with John, as she knew he would disapprove of her choice to visit this old woman.

Mandy's attention eventually returned to Ms. Thelma herself. She noted the wise and kind hazel eyes looking back at her. She had never experienced such intense eyes.   But before she could ask Ms. Thelma about her job and career opportunities, Ms. Thelma declared to her that she was not in the right relationship. "He's not for you," Ms. Thelma whispered, "and he's been unfaithful." Mandy immediately stood up, prepared to leave. "You must have me confused with another client," she demurred. "My John would never cheat on me!" Mandy suspected Ms. Thelma's gaze could pierce right through her head, but the old sage smiled compassionately at her. "You and John have been in a karmic relationship from your past life," Ms. Thelma bluntly revealed. "The relationship was brought back to teach you about The Law of Polarity, while balancing the karma from your past life together in Greece."

Still reeling from the shock of what this eccentric old woman was telling her, Mandy recalled John speaking of wanting to visit Greece. *How would this woman know this,* Mandy asked herself, while attempting to shake off the words she had just heard. Ms. Thelma continued, "Your world is turning upside down to help you land on the proper path of your soul purpose. The animals are waiting for you to rescue them and find them proper homes. And your soulmate will be at your side as you walk this new path because the two of you agreed to this soul contract prior to this incarnation. And by the way, you will be leaving Michigan, never to return."

Rattled and confused, Mandy paid the woman and headed for the door. Before she could close the door behind her, the wise woman, counseled, "Always pay attention to the signs and synchronicities of the Universe. Release your control, my sweet child, and surrender, and the riches of the Universe will fall at your feet."

As Mandy, turned on the ignition, she silently cursed Denise. *How could Denise refer me to this?* Unable to calm herself, Mandy drove a block up the street, out of Thelma's field of vision (she hoped), then pulled over to call Denise. "She told me John was cheating on me, Denise! She must have me confused with someone else." Denise assured her that 95% of what Ms. Thelma had revealed to her had come to pass. As Mandy replayed the outcomes prophesied by Ms. Thelma over and over in her mind, she had a strange feeling in the pit of her stomach. She decided to have an early dinner, try to forget about the past hour, and go to bed early. When she woke up Friday morning, she realized that John had never called her back. There was a text from him saying he was working late and would see her the following night. Excited about their date that night, Mandy reminded herself all day to practice the Law of Attraction.

However, her excitement was short-lived, as later that night, across the table at the Italian restaurant they loved so much, John was breaking up with her. "How can you do this?" Mandy cried. "We've spent four years together and I thought we were going to get married!" John, fidgeting, looked into his glass of chardonnay and declared he had fallen in love with the new account manager his firm had hired three months ago. "Mandy, I've never felt like this before, and we want the same things out of life. We are going to be moving in together next month. I'm sorry to tell you this in public but I thought it would be best for both of us."

Mandy cried herself to sleep that night, feeling like her world had completely crumbled around her. Aggravating the excruciating disappointments of the past few days was a sense of inadequacy that she had failed miserably at the Law of Attraction. As she woke up on Saturday morning, however, she felt a little stronger and decided she would give the Law of Attraction another try. Using the knowledge she'd gained at the seminar, she would manifest her long-desired move to Florida. Posthaste, Mandy started telling her friends and family that she would be moving to Florida to begin her new life. Yet, after several weeks of job-hunting in Florida and no prospects, Mandy began to lose hope. Why were her manifesting techniques not working? As she stared at the flames dancing in her fireplace, the burning embers seemed to remind her of what a failure she'd been.

A few days later, Denise called Mandy and invited her to dinner, saying she had some exciting news to share with her. Depressed and deflated, Mandy decided to go, hoping it would make her feel better. What Denise told her over dinner sent Mandy in a tailspin. "Our company has a job opening in Mobile, Alabama, and you are perfect for the position!" Denise exclaimed. "Alabama? Are you joking? Why on earth would I want to move to Alabama?" Denise reminded Mandy that her job search in Florida had turned up zilch. "Why don't you go back to see Ms. Thelma?" Denise said excitedly. "After all, everything she told you was accurate!"

Mandy scheduled an appointment with the gifted old sage as soon as she could get in. Ms. Thelma immediately assured Mandy that the move to Alabama was a key puzzle piece to the divine plan she had put in place with her Spirit Guides prior to being born. Ms. Thelma taught her about some more Spiritual Laws that must be honored along with the Law of Attraction. "You have successfully applied the Law of Action by moving forward on your desire to move to Florida. You researched the area. You called around and put in resumes. Now you must bring in two other Spiritual Laws to assist you.

The Law of Relativity instructs you to move forward on this relocation to Alabama, choosing to view it in a positive manner. Begin to speak about the new job and the move in an optimistic, powerful way. This energy will begin to shift your vibrational frequency in transformative ways." Seeing that Mandy was following her, she continued, "The Law of Faith must be put into place. This is a time to let go of the control that you think you have and surrender, trusting that the Universe has your back. Love awaits you and surprises are in store for you, but only if you have faith."

As Mandy drove out of Michigan, leaving behind the only life she had ever known to move to a state she had never even been to before, she felt as if she were jumping off a cliff into a river of murky uncertainty. Gazing over at her faithful sleeping cat, Mandy boldly proclaimed, "I am on a mission to discover why I was unable to manifest my dreams and desires when I feel I did everything we were taught at the Law of Attraction seminar. I admit that I feel lonely and afraid, but Ms. Thelma's soothing words play a melody of hope in my heart."

And with those words, she headed south to Alabama.

Chapter 1
My Secret Story

★★★

I'm positive each person reading this book has had both success and "perceived" failure by using the techniques outlined in *The Secret*, the best-selling book by Rhonda Byrne. While I enjoyed the book, and feel that it helped raise the level of awareness and consciousness at the time of publication, I also believe it is time for humanity to explore the deeper spiritual laws surrounding the concept shared in *The Secret*, and why sometimes, the outcome looks different from what you were trying to manifest originally. In other words, the basic concepts within the Law of Attraction and what was written in *The Secret* are valid spiritual laws. However, I have come to recognize that it is now time for us to explore the deeper meanings of these ideas.

It was one of my personal "perceived" failures that prompted me to write this book. Later, I will discuss the reason why I use the term "perceived failure." It is sometimes difficult to share such raw emotions and losses with others, yet I feel it is imperative to discuss these life events so that others may be helped along their personal journey. When we hear or read about another person's experience that mirrors our own, there is an opening for feeling understood. I feel this creates more opportunity for healing and growth. So please join me as I share my very private personal journey with each of you.

Many years after my special wedding day to my now ex-husband, I asked him to list a few of the things about me that made him fall in love. His response: "Oh, that's an easy one. Your positive attitude and your belief that you can attain any goal you set your mind to!" Of course, being a smart husband, he listed many more attributes! But this story is based on that one character trait I have always been proud of. During my life, I have always been able to accomplish and manifest anything I set out to do. Except in one area, that is. My ex-husband and I married on New Year's Eve in the year 2000 on a beach in Southern California. Not only was I joining a life with him, I was instantly a stepmom to an adorable 5-year-old, named Austin. Up until this experience of being a stepmother to Austin, I was unsure of whether I wanted biological children. Austin, who was the best kid anyone could hope for, provided a quick answer to that one for me. I was 36 years old and suddenly, the proverbial biological clock was heard ticking loud and clear.

As I have always done before embarking on the next journey of my life, I began my positive affirmations and visualizations.

I set my intention to have a healthy baby and become a biological mother. *The Secret* had not been published at that time, but I was very familiar with the concept of manifestation, as it had always worked for me. Prior to this time in my life, I had been able to manifest anything I set my mind to. My friends and family were always shaking their heads in disbelief about the things I was successful in manifesting for my life!

I knew how the process of manifesting worked. The key to proper manifesting is to think about and discuss your desire as if it had already happened. I "saw" our little girl! The smile on her face was radiant! In November of 2002, my positive visualization worked, as I found out I was pregnant! I'd never felt that kind of elation in my entire life! My ex-husband and I had created a baby! I shared this news with everyone I could tell, and immediately began searching for a tall building I could stand on and shout my news to the world! Unfortunately, the screaming that followed four weeks later was the sound of wailing. At six weeks pregnant I lost our baby. Desolation crept in, followed by a period of deep sadness and grieving.

After the initial shock wore off, I told myself that many women miscarry the first time. I remembered how important the positive visualizations are to any want, wish, need, or desire. OK, maybe I didn't visualize enough or in the right way. This time I decided to name our little girl. She would be called Jackson, after the town of my birth. I began addressing her by name when I talked to her, as if she were already a member of our family. September of 2003, Jackson was conceived! I thanked God and the angels for bringing us such a special gift. One of the most beautiful experiences a woman may have is the gift of carrying a child in her womb and feeling that connection right away. It's a feeling that is difficult to describe, but most women immediately develop a special relationship with the child growing inside them. There are flashes of daydreaming where you can live an entire lifetime in mere moments. And trust me, I had many such moments as I contemplated how amazing and different my life would be once baby Jackson was born. However, my daydreams and joy were cut short as a meager four weeks later, at six weeks pregnant, the miscarriage pains began again. Devastation does not even start to describe the feeling of loss. For many of us women, there is a shame attached to not being able to bear children. Feelings of inadequacy began to creep into the corners of my soul.

After another period of grieving, I remembered how I have never given up, and always been able to achieve anything with the right belief system and positive affirmations. I just "knew" pregnancy number 3 was on its way!

This time my meditations grew longer and deeper. The special time that Jackson and I shared together was giving me so much hope. I even bought her a beautiful ballerina pillow that would be her first gift from me, her momma. I prayed and prayed. My family prayed and prayed. Our prayers were answered in April of 2004! But once again, six weeks into the pregnancy, our little girl was gone again. As those of you know who have been through these tragedies of lost pregnancies, your world is shaken to the core. Some women become angry at God. You may ask, "Why me? Why do other women bear multiple children and I can't even have one? Where is the justice in women who continue to get pregnant -- often when they don't even want their babies -- while I keep losing mine? Am I not good enough to be a biological mother?" Intellectually, I knew this was not the case, as I had become the best stepmother I could be to then 9-year-old Austin. And Austin really wanted a baby sister. I felt such sadness and hopelessness that I was unable to give him a sibling.

Still, after a while, I declared, *OK, time to get back up, dust myself off, and make sure that my positive visions, affirmations, dreams, and desires are coinciding with my true reality.* I created a vision board. I started reading more and more self-help books about attracting anything you want into your life by using the correct techniques given by each individual author. I meditated. I prayed. I ate healthy. I consulted with the best, most cutting-edge fertility specialists. My ex-husband and I spent thousands of dollars on special blood tests to make sure there was nothing physically wrong. I endured countless procedures, many of them extremely painful, to make sure all my female organs were working properly. I repeated the mantra, "Ask, and it is given," over and over every day. Defeat was not a word in my vocabulary. I theorized that I was given these challenges so that when I held our baby Jackson for the first time, the appreciation would be infinite. Come August of 2004, great news arrived once again! "Wow, this positive affirmation stuff really works!" I marveled. I thanked God for this miracle. I promised Him that I would be the best mother on the planet. But then, at six weeks pregnant, you guessed it; pregnancy number 4 had come to an end. "Why is this happening to me, God? What have I done to deserve this? I have always been an honest, ethical, spiritually solid, good person. It's not fair!" I screamed. It seemed the tears would never stop flowing.

During those three years, I'd suffered severe endometriosis. And after each loss, I had to go through a surgery to remove the relentlessly binding spider webs of tissue. It was like a cancer, in that once it started growing, its tentacles would reach out in search of the next organ to wrap around, as if trying to cut off the life force for good. My gynecologist had informed me that a fourth surgery would have to be the last one, since the scar tissue along with the endometriosis was causing me never-ending excruciating pain. He recommended IVF as our last hope. This was a lot for my ex-husband and me to take in. There was also a huge cost factor involved in this decision. Being 38 at the time was going to decrease the likelihood of success. None of the doctors and specialists could find a reason for my miscarriages. I had the eggs of a 20-year-old I was told, as if this would paint some silver lining to my picture. My ex-husband and I agreed to go forward on one condition. This would be our last attempt at becoming parents together. Due to the daily pain, which was interfering with my quality of life, the next step was hysterectomy. All right, time for the big guns of The Law of Attraction, positive affirmations, positive visualizations, another vision board, and for good measure, acupuncture was added to the mix! This was my time to be a mother! No holds barred! No fear, no worries, no negative thinking.

The day of the egg retrieval, it was music to my ears when our doctor grinned and told us that he had retrieved more than enough perfect eggs. A few days later, on a gorgeous Southern California day, it was time for the embryos to be implanted. Five had made it and were graded the highest quality of A+. We decided to implant three, since this was our final chance of bringing home the gift of a bouncing baby girl. Our acupuncturist was by my side not only with the perfect number of needles placed for greater success, but also keeping me in an ideal state of calm, positive affirmation and bliss. I just knew God would not let me down this time, as He knew this was to be my last chance for motherhood. I now understand that God doesn't decide our fate, or whether we have a baby or don't have a baby. But at the time, I had that belief system.

During the three days of bed rest that followed, I had never prayed so much in my life. I visualized our baby Jackson attaching to my uterus and holding on for dear life. "Hold on tight, baby girl," I told her. We talked about all the things we would do together as we entered the next chapter of our lives while guiding baby Jackson on the first chapter of hers. I laughed, I cried from joy, I made sure I appreciated and enjoyed every moment of being a new mom. I thanked God and I thanked Jackson for choosing me to be her mom. I knew with all my heart that she was growing inside me. And she was, as I found out three days later! "You're pregnant, Jill! The IVF worked perfectly for you!" I knew I could do it. I knew I would be successful at practicing positive affirmations and visualizing what I wanted more than anything. I knew this Law of Attraction concept had given me a fresh renewal on life! I could not wait to tell others of this amazing technique! Imagine how many people this would help to achieve anything their hearts desired!

As fate would have it, I was again given only four weeks to embrace motherhood, as I lost baby Jackson at six weeks. A part of me died that day. I lost all faith. I lost my will to survive. And I lost all my female organs a few weeks later, as they rolled me into surgery for my total hysterectomy.

This was my "secret" story.

After my hysterectomy, it took about a year or two before I could walk into a store and witness a mother with a new baby and not run from the store sobbing. I recall the day when my sister Wendy and her husband David came to visit me with some news shortly after my hysterectomy. As I sat down, the looks on their faces said it all. I knew they were pregnant. I cried, both from happiness at their wonderful news, and sorrow as my losses sank deeper into the darkness of my soul.

When it was getting closer to the time for my sister to give birth to their son, family and friends started asking me if I was sure I still wanted to be in the delivery room. To be honest, I had to give a lot of deep thought to this question. On the one hand, my grief was as fresh as the morning dew, it having been only months since my dream of biological motherhood was stripped away. On the other hand, I had been there for the delivery of my sister's two other children, Payton and Reagan, and I didn't want to miss out on the beautiful miracle of her and her husband's son Tyler entering the world. I'm so grateful I chose love over sorrow in making my decision to be a part of baby Tyler's birth. However, the gut-wrenching pain was still so fresh that I was not even able to stay for Tyler's first birthday party, which took place close to a year after my hysterectomy. As everyone started singing "Happy Birthday," all I could think about was my baby girl and the fact that I never had the chance to celebrate her being born, much less rejoice over each birthday celebration. As the singing grew louder, I felt my throat constricting and truly felt as if I were suffocating. I ran from the party before I caused a scene or did anything to hurt my family's joy.

I have often pondered whether the grief is stronger for a woman who is not able to conceive at all or for the woman who conceives, feels the elation of impending motherhood, then loses her baby. I guess in the grand scheme of things, it doesn't really matter which grief is greater. Both scenarios are losses that will alter the lives of the women forever.

There were days when my sorrow was so bad, it was hard to get through the day. I read books on grief and loss and finally decided to find a grief counselor to work with. On our first visit, my ex-husband and I shared our very personal story of joyous expectation, then loss, in the hope that the counselor could somehow ease our pain. After hearing about all my lost pregnancies, the counselor said, "I know exactly how you feel. I lost three pregnancies myself, but luckily, I was finally able to have a child." My sobbing grew louder. My ex-husband said a few choice words to her, and we left. I couldn't believe someone could be so heartless when their very job was to comfort the grief-stricken. I never attempted grief counseling for my lost pregnancies again. I am sure there are many excellent, caring grief counselors out there who have helped many women heal from their losses; it just didn't turn out that way for me.

To make matters worse, my ex-husband and I were in a very tumultuous custody battle over Austin. Austin's biological mother had found out about my miscarriages and claimed that God knew I was an awful stepmother and therefore, He was not allowing me to bring a biological child into the world. Her new husband's favorite word for me was "barren bitch." She repeatedly told the court and the judges that I was not a mother, and therefore my parenting ability should not factor into the court's ruling. I will never forget the day I found out she was pregnant again, with a bouncing baby girl. I wondered how I could possibly survive in such a cruel universe where the woman who mocked my inability to carry a child to full term could be blessed with another child, and a girl, at that. After all, I had treated Austin as if he were my biological child. My ex-husband and I were finally granted full custody of Austin, who started calling me Mom when he was around 12 years old. Even though my marriage to Austin's father did not last, Austin and I remain very close and he still calls me Mom. One day when Austin came home from school, he said, "Mom, it occurred to me today that God knew you needed a child, so that's why you ended up being a mother to me." My eyes still well up with tears when I think about that sentiment from Austin. And he had no idea that day how very deep his wisdom was. After all, I *had* become a mom. Just because you didn't give birth to a child doesn't mean you can't be a great parent to a child. Or perhaps your parenting comes in the form of animal fostering and adoption. Or maybe you are an amazing teacher, providing parental support to children who may not have very much of it at home. There are myriad ways to offer mothering other than giving birth.

After a lot of soul-searching, I decided I did not want to live the rest of my life harboring these destructive emotions of anger and sorrow. Before coming to this conclusion, however, it took years of inner personal work and struggle to shed the resentment, shame, humiliation, and utter sadness that had become part of my daily life. Sometimes it felt as if for every two steps forward, I had taken three steps backwards. But I have always been a positive person, so I did not give up.

For those of you enduring your own inner demons, possibly resulting from a loss such as mine, I encourage you not to give up on your efforts to work through the pain. It is possible! Reading books about other women's losses and experiences and how they got through them, helped me a lot. Journaling also helped me a great deal. For some people, grief counseling has done wonders. For others, finding a group to be a part of has proven useful.

Yet even after releasing the negative emotions that had become so entrenched in me, I still did not have answers as to why I was not able to manifest a child, when I had been successful at every other thing I had ever put my mind to. So, I went on a quest to find the answers I was looking for. My search led me to various psychics, mediums, past-life regression training, and many meditations. Our journeys are often rugged and winding, yet I can promise each of you reading this book, that if you stay the course on your personal path, the answers will always appear. And for me, as I traveled this road, new jewels of wisdom were provided to me at each fork along the way.

The rest of this book will share my insights on what I found, and the truth that resonates at a deep level for me. I began using Jackson as my last name professionally in honor of my little girl who did not make it into physical form but who lives in my heart forever.

The next chapter of my journey begins here.

Invitation to Explore:

This is a perfect place to stop reading for now and give some thought to areas in your life where you have tried to manifest something and not been successful. Write about your experience and how it made you feel. Did you feel anger, shame, resentment? Did you lose your belief system? What, if anything, have you done to help heal your pain? Simply putting words to paper can be quite powerful in helping us first to see exactly what emotions we are experiencing, and then to help us decide what the next steps are for working through the loss.

Chapter 2
Spiritual Secrets

★★★

After reading my personal story, many of you may suspect that I do not believe in manifestation or the Law of Attraction. This is certainly not the case, as I have spent my entire life manifesting many things, including becoming a published author. For example, years ago, when I decided I wanted to write and be published, I started telling people I was a writer even though the only things I had written at the time were client engagement letters for my CPA clients. Hardly a romantic edge to the launch of a literary career! Regardless, anytime a stranger and I struck up a conversation and I was asked what I did, instead of responding about my current profession, I replied by saying that I was a writer.

I knew to use the technique within the Law of Attraction by speaking of what you desire in the present tense as if it were already so. Within a year or two, I was finally published in a newspaper in Ojai, California. Trust me though, much had to go into manifesting this, including studying, reading books on writing, taking writing workshops, and well, just writing. This conformed to the Spiritual Law called the Law of Action, but I will go into that concept more deeply in a later chapter.

This book is about going deeper than *The Secret* and beyond *The Law of Attraction*. It is about learning to tie the concepts together, with awareness of soul contracts, past lives, and the Spiritual Laws. *The Secret* worked for so many people throughout the years; however, after much study, meditation, and sessions with other reputable psychics and mediums, I finally feel satisfied that I have discovered the deeper reasons why the techniques taught in the book may not work for some of us ALL of the time.

The Law of Attraction is only one of the Spiritual Laws of the Universe! When I came upon many more Spiritual Laws we can learn and apply, I was like a kid in a candy store. I wanted to sample all of them! And when I found out how great they were, and how interconnected they are, I wanted to share this knowledge with others.

What I have also learned is that until we truly know ourselves, we can't possibly know what we want to manifest. Take some time to think back over your life. Would the things you choose to manifest now look the same as the things you wanted to manifest five, ten, or even twenty years ago? Probably not. Why is this? Because as we go through our lives, we have experiences and we learn lessons and we have opportunities for soul growth. Our awareness increases along with our awakening as we begin to ponder thoughts such as: "Why am I here?" and "What did I come here to accomplish?" And hopefully, through this process we grow and begin to awaken to some different and diverse concepts.

Another example of how I personally used the ideas in *The Law of Attraction* is when I realized I would no longer stay the course as a CPA and money manager. I felt satisfied that I had accomplished everything I set out to do in that career, and knew it was time to jump off the cliff and trust that my parachute would open. I began telling people I was a psychic medium. I came out of the proverbial psychic closet even before I started reading for people professionally!

Before we go any further, let me introduce myself. I am a natural-born psychic medium. For those of you who are not exactly sure what this means, allow me to give you a crash course in the work of a psychic, or a medium. A psychic perceives information from someone regarding past, present, and future. A gifted psychic can also communicate with your Spirit Guides. A psychic can give you helpful guidance in areas such as love, career, and even life purpose. A medium receives his or her information directly from loved ones who have crossed over to the other side. A truly talented and ethical medium will be able to provide evidence such as names, dates, descriptions, and specifics of how your loved one passed over. I was given the gift of both psychic and medium, which is both a privilege and a huge responsibility, depending on the day. I go deeper into my journey of being born a psychic medium in my debut book *Mississippi Medium*.

I'm honored to be a member of Best American Psychics founded by Shay Parker. Initially, Shay was a bit of a skeptic herself until she started having some paranormal experiences. While she was searching for someone to help her and provide some answers for her, she found that there were no directories of psychics and mediums, at least none who had been repeatedly blind tested. This eventually led to the creation of her company, Best American Psychics. Shay decided to create a directory in which every member was double-blind tested, with ethics and integrity also required of the members. I was accepted into the group in 2012, won the Social Activism Award for my work with animal rights in 2014, and then in both 2015 and 2016, was awarded the prestigious Psychic of the Year Award.

Even though I was born with the gifts of intuition, prophecy, and mediumship, I did not share this fact with many people. On the one hand, I wanted to live a normal life, study hard, play hard, and have lots of friends. On the other hand, I truly believed everyone could see Spirits. I have always been book-smart, even graduating a year early from high school. It wasn't until many years later that I realized most people around me didn't "know" the things that I knew. It took me a very long time to learn to listen to my intuition, though! One of my Spirit Guides says I had to finally be hit over the head with an etheric two-by-four before I started listening! Ouch!

I believe we are all born with some degree of intuition. Some have it stronger than others, yet everyone can learn to tap into their intuition and strengthen it. It serves us in many ways to increase our intuition. One of the great joys of my life path is being a spiritual teacher to others! I revel in the delight of watching my students become either professional psychics or mediums themselves, or simply use their intuitive abilities to help guide themselves along their chosen life path.

Now I would like to revert to the part about trying to live a normal life! I went to college and became a CPA (Certified Public Accountant). I lived and worked in Southern California where I was a money/business manager for the entertainment industry. An entire book could be written about my amusing experiences in that profession, but I will save that for another time!

After accepting that my dream of becoming a biological mother would not come to pass, my lupus symptoms started coming back full force. I had originally been diagnosed with lupus in my twenties yet was able to get the disease into full remission. Looking back, what I realized is that our Spirit Team will get our attention in ways we may not see at the time, to gently remind us of what we came here to accomplish. The stress from running a fast-paced and highly successful CPA firm eventually caused my illness to return. I ended up in a hospital and came close to death. The stress affected me in a different way than it did my fellow CPAs because this was *not* the life path that I had chosen before incarnating. I had already broken the stereotype of old-bald-male-accountant, so why the hell couldn't I make an about-face, give my weary left brain a rest, and start relying mainly on my right brain? You would have enjoyed being a fly on the wall the day I called my dad and explained to him that the college degree he had paid for was wonderful and all, but I had decided to sell my CPA firm and become a professional psychic medium! Thankfully, I chose parents who were both very supportive of my choices, whether the choice was to pass the difficult CPA exam and open my own firm or jump ship and start talking to Spirits every day. And yes, we do choose our parents prior to each incarnation. This exciting concept will be discussed in the chapter on Soul Contracts.

I have been shown in meditation that we each have a group of Spirit Guides to help us through life. I refer to mine simply as my Spirit Team. And even though I was a very successful CPA and money manager, I quickly realized that this was not my soul purpose. After much meditation, contemplation, and input from other psychics, my decision to sell my CPA firm came easily. It was time for me to take the leap of faith, give up a comfortable six-figure income, and step back onto my true path using the gifts I was born with. It was during this time that I took many classes and became a Reiki Master, which is an energy healer. I encourage everyone to find a reputable energy-healing teacher to study with. After all, everything is energy, and the more we learn to work with that energy, the easier our lives become. I also took tarot classes and learned to use the tarot as a divination tool to enrich my psychic readings. Each class, workshop, book, and seminar propelled me further along my journey and assisted me in finding the life path I had "signed up for," so to speak.

However, I still did not have all the answers I needed and wanted regarding why the tools offered in *The Secret* had not worked for me in becoming a biological mother.

After studying various healing modalities and spiritual growth movements, participating in group sessions with other psychics, having many "conversations" with my Spirit Guides, and becoming certified in past-life regression, I finally became aware of why the instructions and suggestions put forth in *The Secret* may not work all the time. Clearly, the time had come to broaden our views of what *The Secret* and The Law of Attraction do for us personally, while easing into a new awareness that the Law of Attraction is not about greed, or just our own individual manifestations! I am excited to share some of the other Spiritual Laws with my readers that will foster a new level of understanding. We will see how the Laws work in conjunction with each other, while at the same time requiring a synergistic union with our past karma and soul contracts.

All that matters are the here and now, this moment. The Secret and the Law of Attraction suggest that we think, speak about, and vividly imagine the situations and things we want to manifest. You can see that this is taking our awareness to some future timeline and bringing it back to the present moment. It is one of our life challenges to master the concept of leaving the past behind while keeping our feet firmly planted in the present. By the same token, it does not serve us to live in the future, to go through life with the mantra of "what if" and "as soon as." Yet, I do believe the Law of Attraction principles about how speaking your wants, wishes, and desires in the present tense is much more powerful than speaking them in the future tense. Let me give you an example here. Instead of saying, "I want my soul mate -- whom I will meet soon -- to be loving and kind and respectful of me," a much more powerful statement would be, "My soul mate is loving, kind, and treats me with respect. Thank you, Universe, for this gift!" This brings the realization of your desires into the now, into the present moment, and creates an energy surge that helps bring this into reality. In the chapter on The Spiritual Laws, we will discover how to blend the Law of Attraction together with many other Spiritual Laws. We will also explore how our past lives influence our current lifetime, and how important it is not only to get to know ourselves, but to actually fall in love with ourselves (prior to being able to manifest certain things).

Another concept to ponder is this: Faith is another Universal Spiritual Law. There are no accidents or coincidences. An opportunity we all have for soul growth is learning to trust and surrender. We invite our thoughts and words into existence via the Law of Attraction. As well, if we truly believe the Universe will provide everything we need, when we need it, there is unending beauty in trusting and surrendering to this absolute truth. There is such truth and splendor in this quote from Albert Einstein: "There are only two ways to live your life. One is as though nothing is a miracle. The other is as though everything is a miracle."

Most of us quest for knowledge. The type of knowledge and the depth of that knowledge will more than likely fluctuate over time. Gaining knowledge is like rowing a boat down a beautiful stream. You may have a deep desire to row your boat for a while, yet something stirs within you, telling you to pull the boat over to the shore and rest. The experience you had rowing that boat will never be lost. Perhaps you learned new rowing skills, or you experienced an aspect of nature you had never witnessed in the past. Nothing is lost if you decide to increase your knowledge and your awareness over time. This is how these concepts work for us. And then in come the synchronicities that follow. When our awareness increases, we are naturally and suddenly drawn to subject areas and concepts that would never have interested us in the past, or perhaps would not have been understood for lack of awareness.   As we set out on a spiritual quest or path, new doors suddenly swing open to us. We meet new people who generously share their wisdom and experience with us. We learn to take what resonates with us and kindly leave the rest behind. This is a process, much like a caterpillar blossoming into a beautiful butterfly. And everyone's spiritual path and awakening looks different, with various timelines and unfolding in a unique way. The goal is to have no judgment of ourselves or of others as we start to awaken. And even though enlightenment will probably not be realized by most of us in this lifetime, there is a joy and excitement in uncovering universal secrets and truths.

Let's take a moment to think about the word *truth*. Among Merriam-Webster's definitions of truth are: "the body of real things, events, and facts: actuality (2): the state of being the case: fact (3) often capitalized: a transcendent fundamental or spiritual reality b: a judgment, proposition, or idea that is true or accepted as true." Can you now see why your truth may be much different from someone else's truth? And how your truth may even change over time as you evolve? When we take time to really ponder this one word and concept and identify how our own personal truth has evolved over the years, we can more easily have compassion and understanding for those who may not share our truth. There is amazing power and an opportunity to raise our personal vibrations when we practice nonjudgment and compassion, not only toward others, but ourselves as well.

Have any of you wondered why *The Secret* was not published until 2006? Why did this book become one of the best-selling spiritual books of all time when its principal concept was covered and discussed as early as the 17th century? It all has to do with divine timing, as well as the level of awareness of the people incarnated on the planet. Remember that everything is about frequency, a fundamental that we will look at in greater depth in the chapters on The Law of Attraction, as well as The Spiritual Laws. Frequency is a signal which indicates an eagerness and a readiness. Rhonda Byrne must have had teaching and raising awareness as part of her soul contract. Her Spirit Team would have gently nudged her in the direction of writing the book. Just as mine have alerted me to the fact that we as a species are ready to explore the next levels of the concepts covered in this book. In so doing, we find the proper balance between manifesting only for ourselves, in an energy of personal aggrandizement, and manifesting for our species as a whole. After all, we are all connected!

The next era of manifestation for our wealth, happiness, health, and loving relationships will gradually begin to extend to ALL of humanity! It is no longer simply about the "I"; it is about the "We". It is about the greatest of manifestations for Unity and eventually, Divine Consciousness!

Later chapters will also offer ways to discover your personal life path and describe how like-minded souls will begin to gather and form local communities and online groups that support one another on a selfless level of love, understanding, sharing, and growth. These groups are affectionately referred to as our Soul Tribes.

I am hopeful that each of you who read the remainder of this book will experience some aha moments, moments of deep inner knowing. Remembering our authentic selves and the soul groups we were in before this incarnation, helps guide us to the ultimate fulfillment of our karmic missions. As time will reveal, when every one of us strives to manifest good things for ALL our Creator's great children, our Mother Earth will begin to vibrate at a level of energy, not witnessed in quite some time.

Many of you are already familiar with some of these concepts. However, for others, much of this material will be new. Wherever you may be in your awareness, knowledge, and beliefs, I ask that you read this book with an open mind. What I have found both on my own personal journey and in my professional life as a psychic medium reading for my clients, is that sometimes things we are exposed to may not resonate at the time the material is introduced, yet when our psyche is ready to grasp the true meaning, cellular memory will bring the concept back into our awareness and we can experience those moments of understanding. Awareness is like a window to the soul. The deeper the awareness, the easier it becomes for us to peek through the window. There is much wisdom in the ancients waiting for those who seek. Ever increasing awareness is our human right and potential. Open your arms wide and welcome the treasures that await you. You will be forever grateful that you did.

Invitation to Explore:

I invite you to grab some hot tea, and journal about any aha moments you have had along your path in life. Whether you feel you are on the correct soul path or are about to face the proverbial fork in the road, write whatever comes to mind and heart. Journal about some things you desire to manifest for everyone. Some examples may be world peace and the end of wars, the end of hunger, and one of my personal passions, the end of animal abuse and suffering.

Chapter 3
The Law of Attraction and The Secret

***

What is the Law of Attraction? The Law of Attraction is one of many Universal Laws. In simple terms, what this spiritual law teaches is that like attracts like and what you focus your energy on, you will attract to you. This makes perfect sense, as everything is energy and quantum physics has proven that thoughts and intentions do have the power to create our reality. The essence of the law is that if you think positive thoughts, you will attract positive experiences, and conversely, if you think negative thoughts, more negative experiences will show up in your life.

The Law of Attraction has been recognized for eons of time. In 1877, the term" law of attraction" appeared in print for the first time in a book written by the Russian occultist Helena Blavatsky. Since then, this concept has been put forth by many New Age and New Thought authors, from Louise Hay and

Esther and Jerry Hicks, to Rhonda Byrne, when her best-selling book *The Secret* was published in 2006.

Why was *The Secret* so successful? Because we are souls living in a human body. And our human body has an ego and a personality and ever so many physical needs. As humans, we crave things, successes, and people to share our lives with us. Many of us have been taught that our main goals in life are to fall in love, marry, have children, enjoy a successful career, and make lots of money so we can luxuriate in the biggest homes and drive the most expensive cars. But does this *really* have anything to do with why we are here having this human experience? In my belief and experience, the answer is, of course, no! It is surely not! However, that doesn't mean we can't attain all the things we think we may want. But there's one caveat: It must align with our soul's contract.

In simple terms, what *The Secret* teaches is that our thoughts create our reality. Ms. Byrne explains that our emotions, attached to the desired outcome, play the leading role in achieving said outcome. She even advises people to speak about their wishes and desires as if the outcome has already come to pass. I agree that if we are going to practice manifestation, we should think, speak, write, and feel our desires as if they are already in our physical reality. At the same time, we must always remember that if, for some reason, our desired outcome does not come to fruition, there are much deeper and sometimes complicated reasons for this "perceived failure."

As previously mentioned, I prefer using the term *perceived failure.* Let me explain what I mean by this. Just because we are presently unable to manifest something we *think* and *believe* we want; doesn't mean we have failed! In fact, when we can look back and reflect on things in our life that did not manifest, we can usually come to an understanding of why it was not to be.

In fact, for me personally, I have come to realize that my true joy comes from being a mom to animals that I fondly refer to as my fur babies! And as an added bonus, I was given the good fortune to experience motherhood by helping to raise my stepson, Austin.

So, looking back and going through the discovery process of what my soul purpose is, I have been able to reach a level of understanding, acceptance, and even approval for the experiences that have shaped my life.

In Matthew 7:7 we are instructed to "Ask, and it will be given to you; seek, and you will find; knock, and it will be opened to you." The Buddha said, "All that we are is the result of what we have thought. The mind is everything. What we think, we become." What Jesus and Buddha were referring to is the foundation of the spiritual law, the Law of Attraction. The burning question, however, is the much deeper dynamic of why this law sometimes just doesn't work or may not work within the desired timeframe. Have you ever listened to the lyrics of Garth Brook's song, "Unanswered Prayers?" Here are a few lines from this beautiful song: "Sometimes I thank God for unanswered prayers. Remember when you're talkin' to the man upstairs. That just because he doesn't answer doesn't mean he don't care. Some of God's greatest gifts are unanswered. Some of God's greatest gifts are all too often unanswered...Some of God's greatest gifts are unanswered prayers."

That's all well and good, but the question remains: Why would God (or Source) *not* answer our prayers, and how could the positive energy of focused thoughts, feelings, and intentions sometimes fail to bring our desires into being? This is where it can get quite complicated, but I feel it is something that we should be talking and teaching about, so that others don't feel the dejection and depression I did when I was unable to manifest my little girl. The grief from my loss was deep enough without adding the emotion of what I describe as "manifestation failure" to the mix. It is my passion to explore some of the possible reasons that something you are trying to manifest does not come to fruition in the way you had hoped.

This is where the concepts of fate, destiny, free will, and soul contracts enter in, and how they relate to The Law of Attraction. First, let's define these words. According to Merriam-Webster, fate means "the will or principle or determining cause by which things in general are believed to come to be as they are, or events to happen as they do." Per Dictionary.com, destiny means,
the predetermined, usually inevitable or irresistible course of events." From my perspective and understanding, I do believe in the general concept of fate and destiny as it pertains to our soul plan. And to add more flavor to the soup, we also need to throw in soul contracts!

Soul contracts are established between our souls and our Spirit Guides prior to each incarnation. The soul contract is a blueprint which acts as a guide or map for our life choices. I also personally believe in the philosophy of free will, which holds that humans are free to make choices that are not predetermined by prior causes or divine decree. Life experiences do not fit into nice tidy packages with a pretty bow on top. Events are not always absolute. It is within this reality that our consciousness grows, diving deep into the interactions between destiny and free will. If destiny and fate predetermine events to give us opportunities for soul growth, yet we have free will to take detours along the way, can you see how complex things may become when you add the Law of Attraction to the mix?

Have you ever wondered why some people seem to lead charmed lives, yet others have many challenges? There are old souls who have reincarnated many times and young souls who have not experienced many lifetimes. Younger souls seem to have easier life experiences and by the same token older souls have chosen more difficult incidents to delve into during their lives. We can joke with our Spirit Team and exclaim, "What the heck was I thinking when I agreed to this?" Yet, it is important to recognize that our Spirit Team loves us unconditionally and would never have agreed to life experiences that we were not equipped and prepared to handle. However, it is understandable that at times we may benefit by having a heart-to-heart with our Guides and ask for extra assistance during challenging times.

Why is it that *The Secret* sold over 20 million copies and was translated into 50 languages? Because so many of us were obsessed with the idea that we can think ourselves rich, thin, and healthy, *no matter what*. The book claims that if we think angry thoughts, we will manifest events and circumstances that will in turn cause us more anger. I would like to ponder the situations and events in which someone is the innocent victim of a senseless crime. Based on the principles outlined in *The Secret*, this person must have thought angry thoughts of violence, and therefore brought on this crime themselves. I do not share this belief. There are times when karma may be strongly involved in an event. If someone is raped, does this mean the victim had thoughts of violence or hostility and somehow brought this brutality into their lives? Of course not. I believe this spiritual law is very complex and is not as simple as: "Think positive thoughts and you will thereafter be rich and successful and able to afford any house or car your heart desires."

Are the residents of Flint, Michigan, responsible for the toxic water they are living with? If you interpret the principles outlined in *The Secret* literally, an assumption could be made that every person in Flint harbored thoughts of illness and toxicity. The true cause of Flint's water situation is the city officials' poor choice to bring in the city's water from the Flint River rather than from Lake Huron, where it had always come in from. How on earth could anyone claim that every single resident of Flint created their own personal nightmare of sickeningly dirty water? This concept does not make sense no matter how much you think about it. But let's ponder this a little more. What if some of Flint's victims had somehow caused toxicity, whether physical or emotional, to others by their actions in a past life, and had chosen of their own free will to live in Flint and experience the consequences of the poor choices that led to the traumatic events? Perhaps we can expand this concept even further by asking, "Is it possible that some of these residents have an even higher purpose than balancing their karma?" Maybe they chose a life path of service, one that would bring awareness to this injustice, and then crusade to help fight the city and bring clean water to their fellow residents. As you can see, the possibilities are endless.

Rhonda Byrne further maintains that negative thoughts and emotions can even put you in the path of a natural disaster or terrorist attack. It has been noted that this mode of teaching can unwittingly instill fear in people or, even worse, have them blame themselves when some unfortunate event strikes their life. At one time in Southern California, I suffered a massive fire in my neighborhood. I had to wake up in the middle of the night, gather my stepson and my animals, as well as a few personal belongings, and drive away from my home not knowing if it would be there when I got back. I don't believe I'd harbored thoughts and feelings of a calamity, thus bringing this frightening experience into my reality. This just does not resonate as truth for me. Perhaps Mother Earth needed a cleansing in the area where my neighborhood was located. I don't know why some things happen to some people and not to others. No one does. But I do know that there is unfathomable depth and intelligence to everything that happens, which warrants our contemplation and, ultimately, our reverence.

What rings true for me in the Law of Attraction is that we have been given the unbelievable gift to create our realities. We are powerful creators and, collectively, the masters of our universe. Studies have shown that we are using only a small portion of our brain's capacity. What I tell my clients when they want to manifest something in their lives is that the Law of Attraction works in stages. You first have a thought about something you want to manifest. The next step is to write down what you would like to manifest using the present tense. Begin to think about and imagine how this will make you feel.

Within the Law of Attraction is a vortex of possibilities. Just as an automobile has many parts that must work in conjunction with one another before you can drive, your wants, wishes, and desires also have complex and intricate moving parts that must converge in perfect divine synchrony.

I will use an example here of the Law of Attraction in action, along with an entertaining twist. Let's meet Carol. Carol desires a change of scene and thinks about manifesting a move to a new city. In a flash, the white sandy beaches of South Florida come into her awareness as she remembers seeing Miami Beach in a movie. This thought comes in and feels exciting to Carol, and since Carol has studied and read all about the Law of Attraction, she knows she must write down her desire to move to Miami Beach. Carol then starts thinking about what types of friends she may meet when she gets there. She even starts researching the demographics of neighborhoods and condos. Carol finds online forums about community groups and the general energy of the area. Next, she begins to plan a visit to Miami Beach. Can you see how all of this builds the energy? These are all positive and exciting thoughts, combining the Law of Action and the Law of Attraction. (We'll discuss this concept in greater depth in a later chapter.) Let's suppose that after Carol has continued with these positive thoughts and plans, even vacationing in Miami, she returns home and, out of the blue, gets a job transfer to a *different* city. Does this mean Carol was not successfully practicing the Law of Attraction and that manifestation didn't work for her? Not at all! Something actually *much better* happened to sweet Carol! Carol's soul mate/beloved/life partner was waiting for her in that different city! What Carol did by practicing the Law of Attraction was intensify the energy behind the desire for change! And it was this mobilization of energy that nudged her in an unexpected direction, yet it all ended very positively. How about another plot twist thrown in for good measure? Once Carol met her life partner in the city she didn't think she wanted to go to, she discovered that her life partner had also dreamed of moving to Miami! And all of this had stemmed from her initial thoughts of manifesting a change!

I would also like to share a personal story with you about how the Law of Attraction worked for me. I journaled (in the present tense) about my true love and life partner five months before I met my husband Daniel. My description filled two pages with what I wanted, wished for, and desired in my mate, and Daniel possesses them all. Daniel and I have often asked ourselves why we didn't meet earlier in our lives. After all, we both lived in the same small city for four years, went to the same places, and even knew some of the same people, yet we didn't meet until years later. We both have done enough individual spiritual work to understand that we were simply not ready for each other before we met. We still had personal soul growth and exploration to do before we were ready to merge our lives. I thanked the Universe for Daniel before I actually even met him, and I still thank the Universe every day!

While Rhonda Byrne has received some criticism for certain aspects of *The Secret*, I truly believe she accomplished what she set out to do. That is, she wrote with clarity and integrity, and I am personally grateful to her for writing her book. It is my belief that she is certainly one of the pioneers in the New Age Movement. The great number of people who read her book and started focusing on positive thoughts certainly helped raise their personal vibration as well as the frequency of our planet.

We surely could not leave our discussion of the Law of Attraction without including Esther and Jerry Hicks! Esther Hicks channels a group of spiritual teachers who call themselves Abraham. According to Esther, the Abraham teachings affirm our fundamental well-being and help us to recognize and nurture the power of joy in achieving all that we desire in life. Abraham has described themselves as "a group consciousness from the nonphysical dimension." They have also said, "We are that which you are. You are the leading edge of that which we are. We are that which is at the heart of all religions." If you have not been exposed to these inspiring teachings, I highly recommend that you read the books, attend a workshop, or, for starters, listen to the audio recordings of the channeled sessions. The Hickses have been remarkably generous in offering a wealth of YouTube clips from their workshops. The love, wisdom, and power that Esther Hicks has channeled from this group is phenomenal.

There is absolute truth in the teaching that everything in our Universe is based on energy and vibrational frequency, and that positive thoughts, intentions, and beliefs do raise your vibrational frequency. It is my hope and prayer that sharing my knowledge, beliefs, and experiences with others will lead to a deeper understanding of the spiritual laws underlying the Law of Attraction.

When most people are asked why they are wanting to manifest something, whether it is a new house, a new relationship, or a new anything, the answer is almost invariably, "because this new thing will make me happy." Do you agree that finding happiness is the true meaning of life? Is it the goal? What does happiness mean to you? Do material things really make us happy? It is my belief that to know happiness, it must first reside within us. If someone purchases their dream car yet does not possess inner happiness, the euphoria from buying the car will quickly fade and the person will find themselves searching for the next item to buy, or the next accolade to receive, as they attempt to fill an inner void. There is obviously nothing wrong with enjoying material pleasures. However, if we do not feel happy with who we are and practice gratitude for the life we are living, the material objects will mean much less to us. Strive to find your true north of happiness. Joy, gratitude, and a genuine love of life are the main qualities to greet each day with.

I would like to end this chapter with a powerful quote from Gandhi. As you read and digest what he says here, pay attention to the importance of the meaning behind his words regarding our authenticity and destiny: "Keep your thoughts positive, because your thoughts become your words. Keep your words positive, because your words become your behaviors. Keep your behaviors positive, because your behaviors become your habits. Keep your habits positive, because your habits become your values. Keep your values positive, because your values become your destiny."

Invitation to Explore:

Now is your opportunity to journal with a more personal ego-driven goal in mind! Sit down and journal all your personal hopes, dreams, and desires. Remember to write them down in the present tense. I can assure you that this definitely works if your desires are in harmony with other aspects of your life and life path.

Chapter 4
Spiritual Universal Laws

★★★

Our universe consists of Laws or Principles that are meant to govern our lives. Many people differ on how many Universal Laws there are and what they consist of, so for my book, I will be discussing the ten Spiritual Laws that resonate as truth for me, in addition to aligning to and supporting the Law of Attraction.

Universal Law #1 – Law of Attraction

This is the Universal Law most people are familiar with. It basically says that your thoughts create your reality. Like attracts like. Using this law constructively, the focus is on positive visualizations, expectations, and manifesting your dreams and desires. There are many tools that can assist in mastering the Law of Attraction, including vision boards, journaling, visualizations, and mantras. However, as I will discuss throughout this book, this is only one of the Spiritual Laws and to truly master this law, a deep understanding of subjects such as unity, collective consciousness, and soul contracts is crucial, as the true basis at the very core of this law is to bring truth and balance to manifesting in a context of spiritual expansion.

Since I devoted an entire chapter to the Law of Attraction, I would like to spend more time discussing some other Spiritual Laws and how they are interwoven.

The main key in mastering this law, is to know ourselves on a deep spiritual soul level. With knowledge comes awareness. With awareness comes understanding. And with understanding, the clarion call to our true destiny can be heard.

Universal Law #2 – The Law of Vibration

According to quantum physics, everything is comprised of energy, including humans, animals, plants, trees, rocks, water, and even inanimate objects such as furniture. Everything has a vibrational frequency. Thoughts, words, and sound carry a vibration. As humans, we can set our vibrational frequency either up or down. Just because we are not able to see the vibrations of objects with our physical eyes, does not mean that animals, plants, and inanimate objects don't carry an energetic frequency. Research conducted over the years by Dr.

Masaru Emoto proved that the molecular structure of water responds to stimuli such as music, and even to the thoughts and intentions of human consciousness. His bestselling book *The Hidden Messages in Water* details these experiments. Dr. Emoto proved that when positive words were spoken to a glass of water, the water, when frozen, formed beautiful crystals; conversely, when negative words were spoken, ugly crystals formed.

The Law of Vibration is the pillar and the foundation to the Law of Attraction. Before we can attract something to us, a frequency or pattern must be created. Imagine cosmic waves of energy culminating in and around what you wish to have manifested.

To master this Universal Law, we must remember that our thoughts, emotions, and words carry a vibrational frequency, not only within our physical bodies, but in turn throughout the entire universe. Positive words, emotions, thoughts, and actions raise the vibrational frequency of everyone on the planet, as well as Mother Earth.

Try to practice this Spiritual Law in your everyday life. Give great thought to how energy works. Strive to have your contribution to the vibration of our planet be a positive one. Create some uplifting mantras that you will either think about every day or say out loud. Choose your words carefully. Wake up each day and speak at least a few words of gratitude. Focus on bringing alignment and harmony into a positive vibrational frequency in all aspects of your life and begin to witness the magic unfold!

Universal Law #3 – The Law of Action

This Spiritual Law shows us that proactive action is required to bring our dreams, wishes, and desires to fruition. When we take action towards something, a movement or force of energy is created, which helps to activate the Law of Vibration and, in turn, the Law of Attraction.

Let's look at a few examples of the Law of Action in motion. If someone has a desire for a new car, some ways to signal the Law of Action are to begin researching the type of car you want, or taking the car for a test drive.

If you desire to understand a meditation or spiritual practice, action is required to generate the energy around this. By thinking about grasping the foundations of a deep meditation practice, the Law of Vibration begins to create a code or frequency around this subject. To attract this type of spiritual practice into our lives through the Law of Attraction, steps of actually doing something to acquire this knowledge would of course be required. Maybe we drive to the bookstore to discover the perfect book to help us get started. Perhaps we are introduced to a spiritual teacher who specializes in the type of meditation we are desiring to practice.

If the desired outcome is for a mate or partner to share our lives with, the chances of this person randomly knocking on our door is remote -- even if we have practiced the positive intentions of the Law of Attraction. The Law of Action must come into play in every scenario. Joining an online dating site, attending more events with friends, or finally agreeing to be fixed up on a blind date are some examples of doing that which will in turn generate the motion or action. Having a strong sense of self and a solid connection to your higher self will also assist us in putting the Law of Action in motion. If you suddenly receive an intuitive hit or nudge that encourages you to take your dogs to the park, listen. By taking the dogs to the park, you are following the Law of Action, and through this initiative, you may meet the love of your life at that very park!

Universal Law #4 – The Law of Cause and Effect

According to dictionary.com, one of the definitions of cause-and-effect is: "Noting a relationship between actions or events such that one or more are the result of the other or others."

The basis of the Law of Cause and Effect is karma. We reap what we sow. Every effect is a reaction from past actions and intentions. For the most part, creating our deeds and actions around the principles of positive words and behaviors leads to our own receiving of positive words and behaviors. But then why is it that at times we receive the short end of the stick when, say, a random stranger is rude and unkind to us? Basically, that person has created a cause-and-effect ripple for themselves by which they will receive the same energy back from someone else. According to this law, every action has a wave created that affects something or someone else.

I like to think of this law as a wave of ebb and flow, such as the rise and fall of sea levels. The cause of the tide is the gravitational forces of the moon and sun, as well as the rotation of the earth. The effects, therefore,, are the high and low tides and the sea level. We can use this example to help immerse ourselves in the energy of the scales of balance. Every action triggers a chain of events.

One way to grasp the workings of this law is to be honest with ourselves about any areas in which we may subconsciously be creating an effect without consciously recognizing the cause. For example, in my practice as a psychic medium, I have many clients ask me why they have not yet been able to manifest a loving, kind, and faithful life partner, even after they have clearly written down all the particulars of their wants, wishes, and desires. For some of these clients, after tuning in further to their auric fields, I can see fear of intimacy, or lack of faith that such a person with all these wonderful traits even exists! Can you see how the cause of these deep-seated fears has created an effect of the opposite from what they are trying to manifest?

To master this Spiritual Law, it enriches us to practice being kind and respectful to everyone we encounter. And it serves us to conduct our inner dialogues in the spirit of love, trust, faith, hope, and joy. Say this mantra every day: "I am worthy of respectful love" and watch the effects begin to manifest in your life!

Universal Law #5 – The Law of Relativity

The word *relative* moves us to contemplate how things are meaningful only insofar as they relate to other things. Another definition of the word explains that relativity is a state of dependence in which the existence or significance of one entity is solely dependent on that of another. What does all this mean as it pertains to us individually and collectively?

The Law of Relativity holds that nothing is good or evil, right or wrong, hot or cold, unless you are comparing or relating it to something else.

We will always be able to find people who are richer, thinner, kinder, less educated, poorer, or less talented than ourselves. The bell curve shows us that whatever our IQ may be, there is always someone who is more or less intelligent than we are. The meaning or purpose we place on something is relative to how we choose to perceive that very thing.

This is very different from judging. You are choosing to employ a meaning or purpose to compare something in your life. We have each chosen life lessons or soul growth opportunities to experience in this lifetime.

Can you see how this Spiritual Law would, at first glance, appear to interfere with the Law of Attraction? After all, is everyone destined to have the perfect body (whatever that is!), and live in a multi-million-dollar beach house with a Ferrari parked out front, having won the Powerball lottery? Of course, not! Everyone represents a different puzzle piece in this beautiful mystery of life. Some are shaped differently than others, with different colors or forms, yet all are interwoven to complete the tapestry.

As with any other endeavor, the more we remember to use this law, the better our chance of mastering it. For example, we may choose to see the glass as half-full rather than half-empty. We can choose to focus on the good in any given situation. Think about how you choose to view your challenges. We can always spin a challenge into a positive outcome. It really is all simply a matter of intention and perception.

Everything just is what it is. It's as simple as that.

Universal Law #6 – The Law of Polarity

Everything in our world is about balance. There can't be an inside without an outside, an up without a down, a light without a dark. There is a continuum of counterparts and opposites. All that exists, does so on a spectrum, and one aspect cannot exist without the other. There is a beautiful complementarity to every aspect of our lives.

If we never experienced pain, how could we truly appreciate bliss and joy? Without experiences of hurt and disappointment in relationships, gratitude for a life partner who shares so much love and awareness would not be as strong. We have the free will to change our thoughts from one end of the spectrum to the other at any given time – even within the proverbial heartbeat.

We can see how at first glance hot and cold appear to be polar opposites, yet upon further reflection, they are both aspects of the same thing, temperature. Yin and yang are polarizations of the other, yet both are essential. The very duality of the ease and complexity of this law gives us much to think about.

If the Law of Attraction were always successful and our lives were filled with only bliss, abundance, and joy, how could we possibly benefit from soul-growth opportunities and the resulting expansion? We learn from our mistakes. We become better people after our "perceived failures." And for me personally, I learned to love more deeply after experiencing the gut-wrenching pain of grief.

The way to harmony with this Spiritual Law is to learn balance, and to appreciate the challenge of the extremes with detachment. Within every disappointment is potential for greatness. This law exists only in the physical realms. When you find the pendulum of your thoughts swinging toward the negative, stop and take a deep breath and ask yourself, "What is the opposite of the emotion I am feeling?" If you are experiencing a feeling of worry and lack, shift your awareness to an energy of confidence and abundance.

Universal Law #7 – The Law of Free Will

We made many choices prior to incarnating into this lifetime, including our parents, the particulars of soul contracts, and even the astrological energies of our date and time of birth. These choices involved discussion and input from our Spirit Guides, as well as our own consideration of areas we felt needed more experience in the direction of expansion and growth.

During the life review and selection, past lives and karma also played a role in the selection of our gender, the people who would play key roles in our lives, and opportunities for lessons and the fulfilling of soul contracts we made to experience in this life.

The only time destiny or fate comes into play is when it is time for a soul contract or reunion to take place. Fate quietly directs us to being at the right place at the right time.

Since our Creator gave us the gift of free will, this is always in play. We can always choose a specific direction or outcome in our lives. We even have free-will choice when we leave our physical bodies and go to the other side. Our souls always have free will to either expand in our quest for enlightenment, or to stagnate.

How does this Spiritual Law pertain to the Law of Attraction? If we agreed to a soul contract that said we would meet up with and marry someone from our soul group at a certain point in our lives, then fate or destiny will bring that person across our paths. And let's say that our soul recognizes this person's soul immediately and has a keen knowing that the two are to end up together. So, the one person who knows and is ready to move forward begins using the keys from *The Secret* and the Law of Attraction to bring the other person to propose. The other person still has the gift of free will. And by using his or her free will, the choice can always be made not to proceed with or honor the original soul contract. It could be that the naysayer has experienced too much pain and loss in relationship, and therefore suffers a lowered vibrational frequency. This, in turn, constricts the soul to such an extent that their frequency does not allow awareness of the original soul contract.

One way we can attempt to fully cooperate with this universal law is to recognize that the fulfillment of any wants, needs, and desires that we may be trying to draw to ourselves using the Law of Attraction, must not interfere with another's free will, or detract from their well-being.

Universal Law #8 – The Law of Faith

This Spiritual Law teaches trust and surrender. According to Merriam-Webster, the definition of faith is belief in and trust in and loyalty to God; firm belief, even in the absence of proof.

When we step into the energy of lack of faith, or distrust, we are allowing the fear of the ego mind to take control. Many times, this can lead us down a deep dark rabbit hole of despair. And then the Law of Vibration steps onto the playing field and the negative energy thus created vibrates around us and then out into the universe.

Who or what can we have faith in? Most people have faith in a God/Source/Creator, their definitions or expressions of this entity varying from person to person, religion to religion. While visiting the Spirit World, I have been shown that we all have a Spirit Team. This team is comprised of angels and guides who are always there when we call on them. As we enter a conscious relationship with our Spirit Team and learn to blend with their energy, it becomes easier for us to have faith in the role they play in our lives. A knowledgeable Spiritual Teacher will guide you on the path to discovering and deepening your personal relationship with your Spirit Guides.

We also have the opportunity for openness to faith in ourselves. Can you begin to imagine how this task becomes easier the more inner personal work you do and the more you get to know who you are and what you are about? In time, a relationship is formed with your Spirit Guides, and while discovering how to listen to their guidance, you in turn begin to have more faith in yourself.

How do we practice faith? At times, it may feel as if you are jumping off a cliff without knowing where you will land. But if you take this idea and turn it into a positive, there is opportunity for enormous release within the act of free-falling. There is great beauty in the very process of trusting and surrendering.

Universal Law #9 – The Law of Gender

This Spiritual Law teaches us that within both our inner and outer world, we have both masculine and feminine aspects. While transgender people may determine their own gender, and sex may be assigned to an intersex baby, most of us incarnate as male or female. But almost all of us have experienced lifetimes as both male and female. Aided by our Spirit Guides, we make the gender decision for our upcoming lifetime during our life selection process.

When we fall out of balance to one extreme or another, the result is turmoil in our psyches. When we judge another's process based on their individual choices, this also creates an imbalance within our physical bodies. We must strive to embrace one another's freewill choices and lovingly support them on their journey to higher consciousness.

This Spiritual Law goes so much deeper than the outward physical aspects of whether you are representing yourself as male or female in this lifetime. This law supports the Law of Attraction in subtle ways. The more we go within and learn to utilize both aspects of our soul selves, the easier time we have in manifesting. The feminine aspects of ourselves assist us in creating and intuiting. However, the male aspects are also needed as action is required to turn the wheels of motion toward manifesting.

The key to mastering this Universal Law is to maintain an equal balance of yin and yang, masculine and feminine. We are moving out of a male-dominated World and into a more Divine Feminine expression; however, the perfect symbiotic interaction between the two is what we are striving for. The more we begin to experience this sacred merger, the closer we are to understanding the Law of Divine Oneness.

Universal Law #10 – The Law of Divine Oneness

This is probably my personal favorite of the Spiritual Laws, for it resonates with the New Earth, the 5th dimension, the days of the Phoenix Rising. This Universal Law affirms that we are all one, and all connected to the God Source, also referred to as Source. This law teaches us that the days of "I" and "me" are waning, and the days of "us" and "we" are being birthed into a new era of Unity. We are all brothers and sisters.

In Matthew 7:12, we are instructed to "Do unto others as you would have them do unto you." If we strive to live our lives practicing the Golden Rule, and if we can remember that everything we think and do affects everyone and everything else, as we are all connected, then the overall vibration of the planet is raised. The more we strive to honor this law, the more compassionate, understanding, and nonjudgmental we will be.

Why is it that it takes a tragedy for us all to come together in unity and help one another? Can you imagine a World in which neighbor helps neighbor, cities help cities, and countries help countries? That world is now. The midwives of humanity stand waiting to give birth to this new paradigm.

Look for ways in which you can be guided by the Law of Oneness. Our goal as a soul is to realize enlightenment. We have a blessed opportunity within our physical bodies to assist our souls on this quest. Even a gesture as simple as an encouraging smile can alter the energy around us. Many people are serving as links in a chain of good deeds known as "Pay It Forward." The way this works is that when someone does something nice for you, you then choose someone else and do something nice for them. Can you see how amazingly this process works, given that everything is energy? The ripple effect of this notion is mind-blowing, and very inspiring.

It may take humanity several more decades to fully embrace this Universal Law, but I can assure you, the energy of this law is upon us. It's up to you and me to embrace this law in our daily lives and breathe in the love energy of abundance for all, instead of the fear energy of lack. Let us sing the song of compassion and dance the dance of truth.

I hope you've gained a deeper understanding of the many different Spiritual Laws and how their manifestations ebb and flow and work in conjunction with each other. Learning to weave together the treasures from each law to work in synchronicity with each other provides us the greatest gifts.

Invitation to Explore:

Take some time to journal about areas in your life where you can begin to use some of the Universal or Spiritual Laws. Think about some instances in which the Law of Attraction was not successful for you, and journal about some possible reasons using examples from some of the other Spiritual Laws discussed in this chapter.

Chapter 5
Past Lives, Soul Contracts, and Soul Tribes

★★★

Past Lives and Soul Contracts

Have you ever experienced déjà vu when you visited a city that was new to you? Perhaps you felt a sense of belonging and knowing, yet you had never been there before. It is quite common to have these feelings when you are somewhere in this lifetime that you are familiar with from a past life. There is no logical explanation for the emotions you feel, yet you know with all certainty that you *know* this place.

Some people have vivid dreams of their past lives and can remember the details with crystal clarity. Upon waking from these dreams, the dreamer knows that he or she was reliving an experience from another time and place. Past-life dreams are much different from normal dreams. Often, we are shown the particulars of places we have never even thought about. Yet these scenes are quite true to the time and place.

The general belief in past lives has increased significantly over the years, partly because of the success of books about reincarnation. Brian Weiss, M.D., a Columbia- and Yale-trained psychiatrist, was initially a skeptic himself. In his best-selling book *Many Lives, Many Masters*, Dr. Weiss shares the experience of one of his patients, Catherine, who under hypnosis relived events from her past life. Remarkably, Catherine was also able to channel messages from "the space between lives," which contained remarkable revelations about Dr. Weiss's family and his deceased son. This book has transformed the lives of countless readers, and in my opinion is one of those "must reads" for anyone on a spiritual journey.

Some children are born knowing and remembering one or more of their past lives. James Leininger is one of those children. James began providing details from his past life as navy fighter pilot James M. Huston Jr. at the tender age of two. The specifics little James could provide were amazing, including names, places, and very particular details he had no way of knowing. If this story fascinates you, check out the book Bruce and Andrea Leininger wrote called *Soul Survivor: The Reincarnation of a World War II Fighter Pilot* about their son's accounts of his life as Lt Huston, killed in the Battle of Iwo Jima – over seventy years ago!

I have been shown in meditation, as well as when I visit the other side during mediumship readings, that prior to each of our incarnations we go through a process called Life Preview in which we meet with our Guides to discuss what we would like to achieve or work on during the upcoming lifetime. Michael Newton also writes a great deal about this in his amazing book *Journey of Souls*. If you have not read this book, I highly recommend it. Using a special hypnosis technique to reach the hidden memories of subjects, Dr. Newton unveiled some amazing insights into what happens to us between lives. *Journey of Souls* is the record of 29 people who recalled their experiences between physical deaths.

Our souls choose to continue the growth and expansion process through reincarnation. According to Webster, the definition of reincarnation is "rebirth in new bodies or forms of life; *especially*: a rebirth of a soul in a new human body. The soul's quest is for advancement and growth, and to eventually reach enlightenment. Part of the way to realize this is to experience varied lifetimes. As previously noted, in some lifetimes we choose a male body, and in other lifetimes, we choose a female body. Planet Earth is in a third-dimensional frequency now. To choose an incarnation on this planet is both a blessing and a challenge. It is a blessing because of the unbelievable beauty we can experience on Mother Earth. We can share our love both physically and emotionally. The gifts this planet offers us are endless. Yet, due to the density of our Earth, there are many challenges – also known as difficulties -- to work through and overcome as well. Since we each have free will, Earth is a place where we can incarnate to balance our karma and work for soul growth and refinement.

During these life previews, we work in conjunction with our Spirit Guides to make appropriate choices based on experiences from our past lives. In addition to gender, examples of the kinds of choices we make include race and nationality, country and geography, physical characteristics, who our parents will be, and the opportunities for soul growth we will be presented with.

When we go through what is akin to a brainstorming session with our Spirit Guides, what are they going to be assisting us with? In reviewing many of our past lives, they will offer insight on ways we can balance the karma from our past lives while expanding the soul at the same time.

 Among our soul-growth opportunities, we may choose to work on issues related to concepts of money – from poverty to abundance. We may choose to experience certain health challenges. We may choose to teach or increase awareness of societal issues. Or as in my own case, we may choose not to have biological children. As I discussed in Chapter 4 on additional Spiritual Laws, our souls have free will. Free will is the ability to decide which circumstances, among infinite possibilities, we will experience. As humans, we all possess this freedom. The energy of any difficult -- and seemingly negative – instructive intentions that were set by the soul before incarnating   will normally not be avoided by any amount of put-on positivity. Only acceptance, full understanding, and forgiveness can do that.

What I have also learned is that our Spirit Team or Spirit Guides will assist us if we ask them to, but they will *not* assist in bringing about something that clearly goes against what our soul's wish was prior to being born. In fact, they were there and helped us make these choices, so they are certainly not going to betray our soul's choice of growth opportunity.

As a further example of this, we'll use a fictional character named Ruth. When Ruth was participating in her life preview, her Spirit Guides lovingly pointed out many lifetimes in which Ruth was extremely wealthy, yet she used her money and power against others and even allowed people around her to die of hunger instead of sharing her wealth. In most of Ruth's past lives, she had been given an opportunity to learn the lesson of charitable giving, yet in every life, she chose greed and gluttony over philanthropic gestures. For her most recent life, Ruth had chosen, of her own free will, to experience periods of hardship that would require assistance from others. More than likely, in Ruth's current lifetime, no matter how many tools from *The Secret* she uses, she will not win the Powerball. Does this mean Ruth will always be poverty-stricken in this current lifetime? No, it does not. However, her soul chose to experience the karma she had inflicted on others in many of her past lives.

Through training in past-life regression in beautiful Sedona, Arizona, led by a woman I consider to be an Earth Angel, Mary Elizabeth Raines (Rainey to her students), I was shown many of my lifetimes where I had not been "the best parent," so to speak. In many of these incarnations I was a father who left his young children for one reason or another. Many times, I was a mother, who put other things before raising her children. It was finally beginning to make sense why I would not have children during this incarnation, no matter how much I tried to manifest it! This was not done to punish me for the past lifetimes; rather, this was chosen by my soul to balance certain karma that required balancing for my own soul growth. Once this realization came through, all my questions were answered, and any self-doubt released! Finally, I was freed from my perceived "manifestation failure!"

By its very nature, the soul desires expansion. With expansion comes wisdom, and the ability to more or less shed the ego. We as a soul strive to reach a state of enlightenment during each incarnation. What does it mean to become enlightened? One of the more worldly definitions of enlightenment is education that results in understanding and increased knowledge. I personally resonate with the belief that growing awareness not only increases our insight into many areas, it also opens our soul to greater consciousness. Buddhists consider enlightenment as the state that transcends the wheel of rebirth, and is characterized by absence of the desire and suffering of individual consciousness.

What do past lives have to do with *The Secret* and the Law of Attraction? Well, they play a major role in what we can manifest and what we are not able to manifest. So, if you have been unable to manifest something you truly felt you desired, it may benefit you to schedule a past-life regression. It's very important to check the background and training of the regression therapist you choose to work with. Find out where they received their training. Read testimonials to their work or ask friends for recommendations.

There are also psychics and Akashic record readers who specialize in past-life readings. As a psychic medium who places great value on ethics, accuracy, and validation, this is an area or modality for which I recommend a great deal of caution and research. After all, an unethical psychic could very easily weave together a tapestry of untruths regarding your past lives. Make sure you get a recommendation from someone you trust, and then check out their experience, credentials, and testimonials. After all, past lives, karma, and the choices our souls make from lifetime to lifetime are issues that are too important to take lightly.

For me personally, it was the combined results from a past-life reading and many past-life regressions that led me to the realization about why my soul had chosen not to bear children during this lifetime.

I have found it is human nature to beat ourselves up when we are unable to manifest something that is very important to us. It may weigh heavily on our hearts, minds, and souls for years -- sometimes seemingly forever. This should not be. Many inner knowing's are revealed when we learn to use the tools provided to us by our Creator and Spirit Guides. When these realizations dawn, they open up a clearing in which our gifts may shine, and our life purpose or soul path is clear. When we are not saddled with grief and sadness, and we can reach the point of complete release, our lives begin to open in ways we could not have imagined.

Soul Groups and Soul Tribes

Have you, or another family member, been called the black sheep of your family? Do people joke around, that you, or they, must have been adopted or that the stork dropped you off at the wrong house? If this resonates with you, you may have chosen to incarnate into a family that is not part of your soul group.

Souls reside in pods or groups, in which each soul reincarnates with members of their group and surrounding groups throughout many lifetimes. Each soul group normally has between eight and fifteen members. Then there are other soul groups that are connected to your soul group. My Spirit Team has shown me the best way to describe this is to imagine oval pods connected by an etheric cord. Each oval pod contains souls within that soul group. Yet souls from one pod may choose to incarnate with a soul from a neighboring pod if both souls agree they would be a good fit to help each other with their soul growth or to resolve karmic issues.

Sometimes members of a soul group are much different from members of your biological family. At times, a soul will choose to incarnate into a family that is not part of their soul pod to gain knowledge, wisdom, and opportunities for soul growth. If you have chosen to incarnate with someone who causes you great personal struggle and difficulty, this is a sign you are an old soul. A young or new soul would not choose something this challenging.

Souls from our soul groups or soul tribes incarnate with us in various ways in different lifetimes. We each have a group of souls in our group, and I have been shown in meditation that we share lifetimes with souls from our immediate group as well as connecting soul groups. For instance, your husband may have incarnated in a past life as your brother or father. Or a soul from a neighboring soul group may agree to incarnate during a specific lifetime as your mother to assist you in resolving certain matters in your life that have previously challenged you. In this case, you may not feel the same close bond with your mother in that lifetime as you would if a soul from your immediate soul group had incarnated as your mother.

I have given many readings in which a man or woman asked me about their relationship, and when I tune in, I am shown a recent past life as brother and sister. The person I am reading for will exclaim, "I'm always telling my friends that my husband feels more like a big brother than a husband!" When this happens, there is a soul memory of the lifetime as brother and sister. Obviously, these are not the best ingredients for an intimate sexual relationship. Does this mean the relationship is doomed? Not at all. What I recommend in these instances is for one or preferably both spouses to have past-life regressions, so they can "clear" the soul memory of the lifetime when their spouse was their sibling. Another beneficial tool is to find an experienced life coach, Akashic record reader, or intuitive counselor who can assist in locating the soul contract between the husband and the wife. Was there a soul contract showing that they had chosen to experience a lifetime as husband and wife even though they had been siblings in the most recent past life? If there was indeed a soul contract, this would provide more information for the couple to proceed normally, assuming they choose to remain together.

Many times, souls from a soul group may meet up later in life when each member's energetic vibration has molded itself into a more uniform pattern. When this occurs, there is a feeling of instant knowing, instant recognition, and overall love. There is great beauty in having another person truly recognize your soul and see you for who you are.

A soul tribe is different from a soul group. You can be part of a soul tribe without being in the same soul group as the members of the soul tribe. The nature of a soul tribe is to join forces for some common cause. The members of your soul tribe understand you and share the same belief systems you do.

When we meet up with other members of our soul tribes, there is a new energetic vibration that is formed. A frequency is created by the joining together of two or more souls with similar soul contracts. With this new frequency comes an opportunity for each member to help other members tune in to their soul's purpose as an individual and as a group. We will delve deeper into the subject of life or soul purpose in the next chapter.

Another beautiful aspect of meeting the members of your soul tribe is that the divine design behind you connecting with this group is normally for a collective purpose. Perhaps you each have a passion for animal welfare, or environmental issues. Maybe you all have studied energy healing and choose to form a collective. Perhaps you are all psychics and enjoy the camaraderie. Still another group may join forces in communal housing. The options are endless. The key is to watch for synchronicities and signs. Start the dialogue. Our Spirit Team is here to help us! All we need do is ask.

Some of the time, members of our soul tribes do not live close to us. With the advent of the Internet, this has allowed us to participate in our soul tribes all over the world. You may discover that members of your soul tribe mainly reside at some distance, or even in another country.

Many times, we are members of more than one soul tribe. There is nothing more exciting than meeting members of our soul tribes! A feeling of appreciation and gratitude tends to envelop our energy fields. There is never an atmosphere of competition within a true soul tribe. In fact, it is just the opposite. Members within a soul tribe have a strong desire to lift each other up. There is a yearning to help your fellow soul tribe members achieve every success, joy, and accomplishment their soul aspires to.

If you have not yet found your soul tribe, what are some things you can do to connect with them?

First, be aware that your tribe is already waiting for you. Be sure to set the intention and talk to your Spirit Team. Let them know you feel you have learned what you needed to learn from your biological family and   ask for the energy to send out the signals to connect with your soul tribe.

Second, strive for a deep understanding of yourself and what your main interests are. Make a list of all that you are passionate about. Once you have identified your passions, form a group or join an existing group that focuses on the issues you are enthusiastic about.

The more emotional work you have done on yourself, the more likely you are to connect with your soul tribe. This process is not about ego. In fact, it is the exact opposite of ego. It is about getting to know your true self, your soul self, and remembering what you came here to accomplish. Finding our soul tribe coincides much of the time with truly "finding" ourselves.

This chapter would not be complete without emphasis on karma. Given that karma corresponds to the Spiritual Law of Cause and Effect, and that the wheel of karma is always turning, would it not make sense to focus on harmony, as well as contributing to the   wellbeing of our fellow sentient beings? Try not to fall into the trap of evading responsibility for your life by making excuses or playing the victim. Be mindful too that assistance and sharing come in many different forms. Giving someone a sincere compliment cost nothing! Sharing a smile with a stranger does not affect your bank balance, yet the ripple effect can change lives. Let's do our part in creating a world where everyone makes generous deposits to their karmic bank account on a daily basis!

Invitation to Explore:

Consider finding a certified past-life regression counselor and making an appointment. Reviewing our past lives can often shed light on areas in our current life where we may be experiencing struggles. Past-life sessions are normally quite healing as well as enlightening!

Journal about the characteristics of those who will be part of your soul tribe. Have you met any tribal members yet? If not, journal about the passions and interests that you expect these people will share with you.

Chapter 6
Life Path and Purpose

★★★

At some point in our lives, we ask existential questions such as "Why am I here?", "What did I agree to accomplish in this lifetime?", and "What are my talents, and what am I meant to do?"

Many of us at different stages of our lives wonder what direction we are supposed to go in. We are curious about our spiritual (or life) path and what has been divinely orchestrated for us.

As discussed in a previous chapter, before incarnating, we go to what many of Dr. Michael Newton's hypnosis patients refer to as The Ring of Destiny. This is a room our souls go to, where we can preview our next life choices. Once a decision has been made with the help of our guides and our council, the major lessons we are to learn in the next life are set in the form of soul contracts.

This is where the concept of the Law of Attraction appears not to always function as a complementary Spiritual Law. For instance, if we attempt to manifest a lottery win, and we have chosen to learn the lesson of poverty or financial challenges, we will probably not win the lottery. If we attempt to manifest having children, and we have chosen to learn lessons from being barren, more than likely, we will not have children. This does not mean that efforts at manifestation do not work! Most of the time, they do work. However, there are many other Spiritual Laws that work in conjunction with the Law of Attraction.

Most people have multiple missions and life paths. These missions generally become apparent at certain ages or periods of our lives. And at other times, the missions may overlap. It's important to determine whether something you are passionate about is part of your primary life path, or is more of a secondary or ancillary mission. For me, there was a time when I was torn about whether my life path would be as a medium and spiritual teacher, or as an activist for animal welfare. After much reflection and contemplation, I realized that first and foremost, I came here to be an evidential medium and spiritual teacher for many. This does not mean that I view my responsibility to advocate for animals any less seriously than I ever have. It simply means that there are others who *did* choose a primary life path of animal rescue, welfare, and activism. I can still contribute to these endeavors through volunteer work and trying to educate others about the soul nature of all sentient beings.

Where do we begin in our quest to discover our life path or mission? The first thing is to really and truly get to know ourselves inside and out. Consider what you like and dislike, as well as what your strengths and weaknesses are. Just because we are proficient in a certain area, does not mean this is meant to be our life purpose.

For example, my college degree is in business administration. After I moved to Southern California, I sat for the CPA (certified public accountant) exam and passed it on the first attempt, which is highly unusual. For several years, I managed a business management entertainment CPA firm in the Los Angeles area. I then decided to open my own firm, which proved quite successful. I employed several people and had many clients from all over the country. However, as mentioned earlier, I became quite sick and almost died.

I am an excellent CPA and money manager. I earned a great deal of money in that career. Yet, it is not my life path or life mission. It is not what I "signed up" to accomplish. Obviously, this does not mean that others can't find meaning in walking the life path of a CPA or money manager. Of course, they can. Do I regret all the years I spent studying and building my business? No, it made me who I am, and the experience I acquired helps me during intuitive business sessions with my clients. It also helps me manage my personal business more efficiently.

I wanted to share more about my personal journey so that others may be inspired to look at their own lives and be moved to moments of deep reflection. If you have tried to manifest a certain career path only to be faced with hurdle after hurdle or obstacle after obstacle, perhaps this is the universe's way of gently nudging you in another direction. Or perhaps you continue to get sick when you try to remain in a job or career that is not part of your life path.

A helpful tool to use for life-path guidance is the life path number. To calculate your personal life path number, simply add up all the numbers in your date of birth. I will use my mom's birthday as an example. She was born July 25, 1944. You add up all the digits: $7 + 2 + 5 + 1 + 9 + 4 + 4 = 32$; then you continue adding until you have a single digit: $3 + 2 = 5$. My mom's life path number was a 5. A 5 life path number represents people who are flexible, adaptable, and enjoy new environments. People with a 5-life path also make great counselors. This really fit my mom as she was known as a gypsy, moving more times than anyone I know! She craved new experiences and was an amazing person to mediate disputes, as she could easily see both sides of any situation.

There are entire books and courses on life path numbers and numerology, but for the purposes of this book, I will offer a quick reference to each life path number.

Life path 1 – These individuals are born leaders and innovators. Possible careers for life path 1 people are entrepreneur, manager, politician, and senior managers.

Life path 2 – People on this life path pay attention to details, enjoy balance and equilibrium, and are inclined toward the mystic. Writers, artists, meditators, psychics, and child psychologists are commonly found on life path 2.

Life path 3 – My life path number is a 3. This path is all about creativity and helping others. It is a highly empathetic life path number which often includes a mission to inspire and uplift others. Publishing and media fit into this category. A preponderance of actors, artists, writers, public speakers, and psychics share this life path number.

Life path 4 – This life path number is associated with security, responsibility, and plain hard work. Family and legacy are important to life path 4 people. Accountants, bankers, financial planners, engineers, architects, real estate moguls, and tax lawyers may all fit in this category.

Life path 5 – As in the case of my mother, life path number 5 represents people who are flexible, adaptable, and eager to experience new environments. Those along this path tend to dislike routine, and prefer jobs and careers involving travel or the outdoors. Counselors, firefighters, construction workers, and those who must travel in their careers are often among the fives.

Life path 6 – The path of these individuals is about peace, harmony, and healing, as well as a connection to music and/or art. They are also great nurturers and are intuitive. There is an affinity with children and animals. Life-path professions may include teacher, healer, writer, artist, and interior decorator.

Life path 7 – People on path 7 are sometimes misunderstood, as they prefer the mysterious and may require a great deal of alone time. This desire for solitude may facilitate connection to higher realms if the person learns to meditate and tune in properly. Sevens are problem-solvers and highly intelligent. Mathematician, chemist, detective, doctor, psychic channel, or scientist would all be great choices for a life path 7.

Life path 8 – Individuals born under the influence of life path 8 normally make great leaders. They are also able to manage large sums of money. There is an affinity towards power, and business skills are usually outstanding. Career options would include business leader, accountant, financial advisor, and high-ranking law-enforcement officer.

Life path 9 – Guiding and inspiring people born under life path 9 is a great deal of idealism. Most are old souls that chose to incarnate to help humanity in some way. Many are natural-born volunteers and humanitarians. Mother Teresa was a life path 9. Social work, teaching, diplomacy, and intuitive counseling would all be good career choices for a life path 9.

If numerology interests you, you can find many books written on the subject. I am certainly not a numerologist; however, I very much resonate with the accuracy of the information that comes from working with numerology. This description barely scratches the surface on this ancient esoteric modality.

Many spiritual practitioners find themselves called to assist people in discovering their true path. Some people benefit from past-life regression or even life-between-life regression, as the sessions prove quite beneficial in determining the challenges and progress of our souls. According to The Newton Institute, a life-between-life session is a deep hypnotic process, developed over many years, designed to heighten awareness of one's soul self and Spirit Guides, thereby awakening an understanding of immortal identity. Many people have received great insight from participating in these regressions. I have personally benefited a great deal from them, with past-life regression training and certification guiding me ever deeper.

The more we tune in and get to know our authentic soul selves, the more easily we can access and remember what our life mission is for this lifetime. Studying intuitive development with a qualified teacher has assisted many people in getting to know themselves better. One of my personal missions in this lifetime is as a spiritual teacher. I created an online academy, Intuitive Compass Academy, so that anyone, located anywhere in the world, could participate in my classes. I can't tell you how many of my students over the years were finally ready to step into the energy of who they are and what they came here to do. I also created an in-person academy, Mississippi Academy for Psychic and Mediumship Studies, and people are traveling from all over the country to attend. I have been told by other seers that I am a catalyst of sorts, to promote and assist others on their journey.

My work is another example of paying attention to signs from the universe. I had absolutely no plans or intention to teach intuitive psychic development. None whatsoever. Many years after I became a professional psychic, some of my clients started asking me to teach them about intuition. I smiled and went on with my day. Remember, one of my Spirit Guides likes to talk about me sometimes needing to be hit over the head with an etheric two-by-four before I pay attention! After a period of time and many, many requests, I started thinking about developing a program. Mind you, I was still simply *thinking* about it! And then, I was at an event with some other colleagues, and Marc Lainhart, a fellow Best American Psychic colleague, handed me a polished crystal rock with the word's "teacher" written on it! OK, the message finally sunk in! I began writing the course material and scheduled my first class. I am so grateful for the gentle and not-so-gentle nudges along the way.

Looking back, I now recognize that my higher self was always trying to tell me I am a teacher. When other kids my age were playing with Barbies and baby dolls, or even playing doctor, I was playing teacher. I had a chalkboard with all my stuffed animals lined up for their lessons. Nothing like having a captive audience full of stuffed bears, dogs, and bunnies! All joking aside, can you see how my nine-year-old self was already "in the know" about one of my soul contracts? Think back to your childhood and see if there were any clues as to what your life path would be.

At times, I have had clients tell me that they believe they are too old to change directions. We are *never* too old to adjust our path! Some of us need to have had particular experiences preparatory to taking the steps toward our life purpose. Others may have to honor multiple soul contracts, tailored to various chapters of their lives. And then there are those of us who require a great number of signs and synchronicities, or even the extreme of a near-death experience before we alter the direction of our lives. Whatever your personal circumstances, it's important not to beat yourself up or harbor regrets. Every encounter and event in our lives happens in order to help our souls expand. Knowledge and wisdom from our past provide an endless stream of power that expands our awareness.

There is such eloquent beauty in the serene confidence that comes from following your calling. By sad contrast, the static frustration of those who choose to avoid the risks involved in pursuing their hunches and ideas is painful to behold.

Great benefit is in store when we explore our dark or shadow side. It was psychiatrist Carl Jung who named our dark side the *shadow*. According to Wikipedia, the shadow may refer to (1) an unconscious aspect of the personality which the conscious ego does not identify, or (2) the entirety of the unconscious, i.e., everything of which a person is not fully conscious. In short, the shadow is the "dark side." To truly know oneself, we must recognize and own the dark side of ourselves as well as the bright side. Again, this goes back to the Law of Polarity, which we discussed in Chapter 4. According to Jung, "That which we do not bring to consciousness appears in our lives as fate." In a talk about accepting the darkness in self and others, Alan Watts explained: "Jung taught that the task in life which thus confronts everyone, is to become conscious of and integrate one's shadow into one's conscious personality, accepting it with open arms not as an abhorrent aspect of one's self, but as a necessary and vital part of one's being." Getting to know our shadow selves propels us to the realization of our goals. There are amazing books to read and courses to take that help us work with our shadow side. Moment-to-moment inquiry into our true motives is especially helpful.

Now is a perfect time to talk about trust and surrender. We looked at trust in Chapter 4, in the section about the Law of Faith. What is trust? According to one definition, it is "a firm belief in the reliability, truth, ability, or strength of someone or something." In what or in whom do you have trust? Do you trust yourself? Do you trust that there is a higher power or God or Source? What about your Spirit Guides? Do you trust that you do have personal Spirit Guides that are always there to guide you? As I have mentioned several times, I love teaching intuitive development and helping people understand the role of their Spirit Team, as well as acquainting them with their own guides and higher self. Vast resources of wisdom and knowledge are available from our all-loving guides.

This is where surrender enters the mix. Merriam-Webster tells us that one definition of surrender is to give up completely. I know that for myself and for many of you, control is one of life's toughest lessons. To be in control gives us a feeling of invulnerability and power. At times, it may even seem like a drug, in that you may struggle with actual withdrawal symptoms when you feel you are losing that control. What I have learned is that we are rarely in control of anything other than our free will.

When we try to control another person, it normally backfires on us. At this point we can still stop, back up, take a breath, and understand that even though we may have succeeded in controlling that person, it is always a lose-lose situation of jailer and jailed. Neither person has gained anything.

What about when we try to use control to navigate the path of our lives? How has that worked out for you? I know for myself, not so well. For years, I was under the false assumption that if you had a desire or an accomplishment that you yearned to achieve, the best way to succeed was to plow forward, full steam ahead! I was so heavily addicted to my *drug* of control that I often failed to see the caution signs along the way. Looking back, I remember times when the red light signaling me to STOP was flashing so brightly, it was probably seen in outer space! Yet, I raced forward at lightning speed, missing the signs and signals from my Spirit Team that should have been obvious. Have you endured similar dynamics in your life? Are you currently plowing forward so quickly and aggressively that you are missing key signs or landmarks along the way?

Let's play a game together. Let's celebrate the fact that you have just won the Powerball lottery. Congrats! Once the partying has died down, take some time to journal about the things you intend to buy. Will you be getting things for your friends and family? What will you buy? Are you going to quit your job? How and when will you notify your bosses? Do you think you might start a business? If so, what type? Are you interested in devoting your now-free time to volunteer work? If so, what type speaks to you?

Your lottery journaling will reveal a great deal about who and what is near and dear to your heart. Some of your answers will unambiguously show how important your current job is to you. If the first response out of your conscious mind was, "Hell, yeah! That job is history!" this of course tells you that your current work probably doesn't resonate with your life purpose. Or you may be in the correct field, but simply with the wrong company. Don't wait to win the lottery to make these changes! In the words of Joseph Campbell, "Follow your bliss!"

If you got excited thinking about a certain business you would buy or start, let this be a key to unlock your soul's hidden passions. Begin to research the business and start writing a business plan. Sometimes, the very act of writing a plan, either attracts the energy of the business to inform and invigorate your life sooner than anticipated, or it shows you a different direction that is more beneficial to you.

How many of you thought about volunteer work or charities you would love to be more closely involved in? Contact these nonprofits and ask what is needed. See if any of their needs fit in with your current schedule. There are people who love animals but don't have time to devote to caring for them full time. I know some people in this situation who contribute their time driving the animals to other areas, so they will have greater chances for adoption! Can you see this is an important part of the wheel?

These exercises will illuminate your life path and expedite your journey. When this lifetime is complete, what do you wish to be remembered by? What would you like your legacy to be?

The key to evolutionary strides along your life path is to really get in touch with your soul and surrender, so that events may unfold as they are supposed to. I encourage each of you to continue the practice of manifestation in your lives, while also learning to surrender to your soul's master plan.

Invitation to Explore:

Read a book on the shadow self or find a course that helps you explore your shadow. Consider studying intuitive development through courses or books. Using your life path number, deepen your understanding of its energies by reading books and watching YouTube presentations about numerology. Research certified past-life and/or between- life therapists with the goal of further discovering your life path. Spend time considering the "lottery game" we just played, and journal about your results.

Chapter 7
Frequency and Manifestation Magic

★★★

Everything is comprised of energy or waves, including human beings. Quantum physics teaches us that everything is energy, including people, animals, trees, rocks, and even water. We are not just our physical bodies. We also have an etheric body, an emotional body, a mental body, and an astral body. Our thought patterns as well as our words, and even actions, affect our energy vibration. As mentioned in the last chapter, past-life memory as well as events from earlier in our lives can affect our energetic signature.

I have discovered through experience that it is much more complicated to discover your life path or soul essence when your energy field is low or vibrating at a low frequency. This is a complex subject, so for the purposes of the concepts in this book, I am going to focus on tools to help increase your frequency.

Thought patterns create a wave or frequency that ripples out from your energy field. Strive to generate ideas and beliefs that increase your personal vibrational frequency, as well as that of the people around you. As we walk confidently toward the fifth dimension, it is vital for us to remember that each of us vibrates as part of a collective. This will be discussed in depth in the next chapter. The focus of this chapter is to set your intentions to keep your frequency elevated in order to assist Gaia in her ascension, while also raising group consciousness.

Positive thinking is a process that leads your mind to embrace joy, happiness, success, and positive results. We are inherently predisposed to surround ourselves with positive- thinking individuals. Just being in a positive-thinking individual's energy has the power to uplift our energy.

By the same token, those who think negatively teach their minds to accept fear, worry, unhappiness, and negative results or outcomes. My husband, Daniel, ever bringing humor into the mix, loves to remind people not to use stinkin' thinkin', as this contributes to our energy vibrating at the lower end of the frequency spectrum. Zig Ziglar, who preceded Tony Robbins as a motivational speaker, originally coined the phrase *stinking thinking* in his seminars. He taught that stinking thinking did not provide the right formula for good things to manifest.

There are many ways we can self-sabotage by allowing in the negative self-talk. One example of negative thinking and programming is when we use the word *always* or *never* to describe a situation that we have encountered. For example, let's say that Julie is turned down for a job position she applied for. The negative way to express this disappointment would be for Julie to say, "I'm never hired for the jobs I want," or "They always choose someone else for the position I really wanted." What would be the wiser choice of words in this situation? Julie could say, "I'm disappointed that someone else was chosen for the position; however, I trust that the Universe has my back and has something even better in store for me!"

Negative thought patterns may also run amuck when we verbalize regretful feelings – *I shoulda, woulda,* and *coulda.* The energy of regret can be a hazardous road to travel. What is regret? Regret is fervently wishing you had done something differently. Life continually presents us with choices. We may choose to act and pursue an opportunity, or to ignore or reject the opportunity. There are those who blithely jump from an airplane without giving thought to whether they have a parachute to help in their descent. Conversely, there are those who shy away from opportunities due to fear -- fear of failure, fear of rejection, fear of disappointment, etc. They may live with the proverbial deer-in-the-headlights look deeply etched on their faces. What I have found to be the highest-vibrational decision arises from the spectrum between these two extremes. When we tune in to an opportunity while in the greatest alignment with our Higher Selves, we receive proper clarity on whether to jump or not. Trust me on this! When we are in that space of trust, flow, and ease, the Universe will not allow us to jump without our parachutes in tow!

It's important for us to remember that, as imperfect humans, we will sometimes make decisions while we are not in perfect alignment. At such times, it is imperative that we not buy in to the energy and notion of regret. Regret takes us out of the now and into the nonexistent fruitlessness of *woulda, coulda,* and *shoulda.* Regret takes us down a dark road of guilt and shame. Guilt and shame work tirelessly to keep our energy hovering at the lower end of the frequency spectrum. What we can do, however, is learn from our mistakes. We can choose to work through our limiting beliefs and fears. We can embrace change and new opportunities as long as we know deep in our soul that we are not being reckless in our behaviors.

Be very careful about labeling yourself or others in less than flattering terms such as stupid, loser, broke, unlucky, or fat, even if you say these words jokingly or in jest. When I have lovingly pointed out to someone that they are using lower-vibrational words, many times the response will be, "I'm just joking around." The Universe records every thought, word, phrase, and action. No disclaimer of comedy will stop the Universe from recording every word you say!

I even invite you to change the way you say, "I'm sorry." It is not in your best interest to put that energy out into the Universe! After all, what is the definition of sorry? *Sorry* has the connotation of being worthless, and creates an energy of regret, the negative influence of which we've already discussed. Try to get in the habit of saying "I apologize" instead of "I'm sorry." This may seem silly, but I promise that you will notice a shift in your energy field when you begin making these small changes in the words you choose.

People can easily become addicted to negative thought patterns and negative words. As we progress along the path to ascension, we find ourselves unable to be in the company of these types of individuals for long periods of time, if at all. They are toxic to our physical, emotional, and spiritual well-being.

Most of us accept these concepts, as we are still living in the third-dimensional earth plane. The key is to make a point of practicing positive thinking in your daily life. Find affirmations that appeal to you and practice saying them every morning before you begin your day. Some examples are, "I am blessed," "I am pure love," "I am abundant," "I am grateful."

All living beings are affected by the energy of their environment; however, those who have chosen to become aware and raise their energetic vibration are even more affected. It is of vital importance for those on a spiritual path to be in an environment that is geared to emotional protection and relaxation. I make sure to tell my students that as they walk through the doors of expansion, awareness, and awakening, they can never turn back. Expanding our awareness changes our frequency in a very positive way. However, I would be remiss in not explaining the changes that occur with the choice to awaken. Environment is critical to those who walk the path of expansion and awareness. Pre-awakening, you may be able to tolerate low- vibrational people and environments. Post-awakening, being in the energy of low-vibrational people can be pure torture on the auric field. It is important that we not stand in judgment of those who have not awakened, or who still choose lower-vibrational words, actions, and lifestyles. It is certainly not our place to judge. But it is our responsibility to exercise discernment, and to walk away from these toxic people and environments with love and grace.

All energy can be balanced with a combination of positive thinking, which raises your vibrational level, and working with a qualified energy practitioner to release past trauma. This, however, is an ongoing, lifelong challenge, so be gentle and loving with your evolvement over time.

As we begin to follow these concepts and learn to honor our connection to Source, our energy begins to vibrate at a higher frequency. Another wonderful way to increase our vibration is to embrace the concept of Unity and Divine Consciousness, instead of the more common notion of separateness and division. We are all One and part of Source. I discuss this concept in great detail in the next chapter. When we practice unconditional love, joy, acceptance, compassion, and tolerance, we in turn raise our vibrational frequency, as we are all connected.

After you have successfully raised your vibration, there are many areas of your life where you will notice great change. I am passionate about discussing all the positive changes that occur when our frequency rises.

Control

When we raise our vibrational frequency, our need to control everything that happens is greatly diminished. If you stop and think about this, you'll see that control takes a great deal of time and energy. And it's certainly not a sexy word! Control is governed by the ego mind, and actually limits outcomes. Control is dominated and directed by fear. By contrast, surrender allows for limitless possibilities. Surrendering requires absolute faith in ourselves, our Spirit Team, God, and the Spiritual Laws of the Universe. This is not always the easiest path to navigate. But if we train our minds to focus on the fact that we are indeed co-creators of our Universe and our lives, this empowers us to embrace the ease and flow of allowing the Divine to beautifully orchestrate the highest and best outcome in everything we do. Breathe in the energy of this for a moment. Feel it in the depths of your soul. Trusting to the point of surrender is one of the greatest gifts you can give to yourself.

Joy

When we offer positive words, thoughts, and actions, we experience joy more frequently. Other words for joy are delight, ebullience, elation, and happiness. These are such light, fun words. When I ponder the emotion of joy, I am made aware that many times humans feel guilty when they experience true joy or bliss. Why is this? If someone has been made to feel unworthy, the radio dial in their minds may be stuck on the station that tells them they don't deserve joy. Or maybe they play the station that warns them that when goods things happen, the other shoe will surely drop soon. Or possibly, being depressed and down all the time has brought them more attention. Practice being in a state of joy. Make time to play. Of the thousands of readings I've done, one of the main messages from our loved ones on the other side is this: "Have fun! Play more!" Most children have not been programmed to question or abandon their joy. We can learn a lot from children. What I can tell you is this: The more you focus on raising your personal vibration, the more comfortable you will be wearing the bright attire of joy.

Environment

When you raise your vibrational frequency, you begin to notice that you need more quiet and alone time and simply cannot be in certain places where you used to go. My psychic colleagues and I joke about putting our body armor on when we must go into the big-box stores! For me personally, one thing I notice as my vibration continues to shift higher is that I can't tolerate noise like I used to. By contrast, science has found that listening to music at a 432 Hz helps shift our consciousness. My personal belief is that music tuned to 432 Hz helps align us with the heartbeat of the Universe.

Nature is a free gift that helps us to unwrap our emotional blockages from the discord and hectic pace of our current world. Some people joke about tree huggers, and when they picture true tree huggers, 1970s hippies come to mind! But tree-hugging is beneficial to all of us. Science has proven that hugging and speaking kindly to trees, and even being in the vicinity of trees, has a positive effect on our physical and mental well-being. Many spiritually minded people I know receive great benefit from walking barefoot on the earth. Connecting in this way to the raw grass and dirt can bring us a sense of safety, calmness, and serenity. As you raise your vibration, make sure you schedule time to unplug and commune with nature. Your aura will thank you!

Patience and Compassion

When you raise your vibration, your patience is improved, and you offer more compassion. Practicing more compassion for others is a wonderful way to shift your own vibration. Patience is certainly a virtue. When we are not rooted in the energy of patience, we tend to be anxious and nervous. These are lower-vibrational behaviors. When we learn to feel and express true patience, we remember that the opportunity to see the joy in every moment is ever before us, even if that opportunity happens while we're sitting in traffic or standing in a long line at the supermarket. (Especially then!) It is all about shifting the story we tell ourselves. In one of Edgar Cayce's channeled readings, he says, "When patience becomes an active principle in our lives, we rise above the boundaries of time and space. Our finite mind and our human side hold us in the dimensions of time and space, but we have access to our infinite mind. Our Christ-like side can and will lift us beyond time and space." For me, this is still one of my greatest challenges. I tend to feel justified and comfortable with being impatient. However, this is an area in which I'm determined to pay attention and make progress every day! If this is also a challenge for you, please join me in setting the intention to remember the above words of Edgar Cayce.

Intuition

When you raise your vibration and learn to stand in perfect alignment, your intuition is greatly enhanced; therefore, you attract more people into your life who are living in truth. You have a greater chance of connecting with your soul tribe. You start to recognize that there are no coincidences, so when you experience synchronicities, you gratefully acknowledge them as signs from the Universe. I am adamant in my belief that everyone would do well to participate in a psychic or intuitive development program. A good intuitive development program teaches the difference between the expressions of Higher Self and ego. It describes the auric field and how to work best within that energy, as well as how to connect with your Angels and Spirit Guides. The Universe is an inconceivably magical, mystical place. One of the keys to a loving and productive life is to learn to tap into this magic. When we refine and strengthen our intuition, we more mindfully embrace obstacles and recognize the opportunities hidden within them. This does not mean we do not allow our human emotions of disappointment, frustration, or sadness to express themselves. These emotions are essential parts of being a human being. What it does mean is that once we process emotions based on a perceived obstacle or a potential missed opportunity, we then adjust and shift this energy into a higher spiritual perspective. The fourth density is a frequency in which we can begin to step out of the ego mind, embrace creativity, and allow occurrences we perceive as negative to shift into increasingly positive expressions.

What does this mean exactly? We consciously take a disappointing situation such as a job loss, a house falling through escrow, a relationship collapse, etc., and offer the situation up to the fourth dimension, allowing it to take on a different meaning and appearance. In order to do this, we must surrender and trust, centered and in alignment with our Higher Selves. It may take a few hours, a few days, or even a few months for the new reality to present itself to us as an opportunity. When we are in the lower-density energy of disappointment, anger, frustration, or victimization, it is nearly impossible to imagine that the situation at hand could ever offer new and different possibilities.

When we learn to tap into this Divine Generosity, it's like opening up a gift all the time! We simply must get out of the way and stop trying to paint the scenes to match our third-density ego wants and desires and moods.

We each have a conduit straight to the Divine. When we learn to tap into and trust our intuitive guidance, inspiration and knowledge tend to flow in a seamless and effortless manner.

Relationship Changes

When someone does not vibrate on a level that matches your truth, you are more prepared to release them from your energy field. As your vibration shifts and changes, some of your friends and family may actually start feeling uneasy in your presence. Your joy, trust, and compassion for all tends to make them feel uncomfortable within themselves. Sometimes long-term friends, lovers, and spouses suddenly walk away for apparently no reason. They may not even be able to explain it to themselves. It is important to remember that when people leave our lives, this creates more space and energy for those of like minds to take their place. As your vibration rises, it is as if you are sending a beam of light or radio signal to those who can recognize this radiance. Strive to be that beacon of illumination and you will open doors to relationships you never dreamed possible.

This book is about going beyond the Law of Attraction. This chapter focuses on energy, vibration, and frequency. Once we understand the concepts of consciousness expansion, awakening to the truth of the Universe and weaving in the other Spiritual Laws, we are in proper alignment to practice manifestation magic.

Let's take a look at the difference in the energy from the original Law of Attraction taught in *The Secret*, to the more expansive manifesting from a higher and deeper perspective.

Old Paradigm: Matt decides to manifest using the teachings from *The Secret*. Matt declares, "Universe, I am the happy owner of a beautiful new Ferrari!" Matt is certain that a Ferrari is the car for him! Matt does not take into account any soul contracts or infinite knowledge provided from his Spirit Team.

New Paradigm: Matt has finished reading *Secrets of the Secret*. In addition, he has spent time studying spirituality and the deeper meanings of the Universe while learning to tap into his intuition. He decides to employ manifestation magic using the techniques in this book.

So instead, Matt is inspired to say, "Universe, I would love a new car, and I trust the Universe to deliver it to me with the greatest of ease and in the highest and best way." Matt understands that in previous lives he amassed great wealth and chose to be quite greedy. In this lifetime too, he has acquired financial abundance; however, he now chooses to share his wealth by taking care of animals and feeding the homeless. Matt's Spirit Team knows that a Ferrari is not the best option for carrying food to people and animals, nor is it the best vehicle for transporting animals who need help.

In the aura of Matt's trust and surrender, someone tells him about an almost new beautiful SUV that just happens to be in his price range of comfort. As Matt drives home in his nearly new luxury SUV, he marvels and revels in gratitude about how amazing manifestation magic is. Some would argue that he failed at manifesting a Ferrari. Matt, by understanding the concepts in this book, would tell you that his role was to co-create something much better.

Invitation to Explore:

Take some time to reflect on ways you can shift your awareness to the true beauty of manifestation magic. Delve into some areas in your life where you can employ these concepts while releasing any remaining "in the box" constraints from the old Law of Attraction paradigm.

Chapter 8
Collective Wisdom
★★★

What is collective wisdom? According to Wikipedia, collective wisdom is shared knowledge arrived at by individuals and groups, used to solve problems and conflicts of *all humanity*. Drawing from the reservoir of Universal Truth, the point of collective wisdom is to make life easier/more enjoyable through understanding human behavior. The wisdom is not used for "self" to bring in wealth, abundance, soulmate love, or fame. The wisdom is understood and acted upon for the benefit of all humanity! How beautiful is this? Imagine for a moment that every person on Mother Earth understood and practiced collective wisdom.

Some of you may be wondering if it is wrong or ineffectual for you to continue to pray, use mantras, and practice positive visualizations. Of course, it's not wrong! In fact, these practices go hand in hand with the bringing in of collective wisdom. There is absolutely nothing wrong with wishing for abundance, true love, a fulfilling career path, and financial success. However, it is very important to understand that now that the Phoenix Days are upon us, our current financial system will be changing from what it is now. It is my belief that our current system is unsustainable. My prediction is that more people will begin bartering as focus shifts to smaller communities working together for the greater good of everyone in that community. You can already see this dynamic at work with the rise of community co-ops and local farmers markets. Community-based trade provides a beautiful opportunity for us to get back to the basics of connecting with each other on a deeper level. The ripple effect of these small changes will be far-reaching.

The balance of karma is always in play. Too many people bought into *The Law of Attraction* and *The Secret* solely out of greed and for personal gain, without also considering the many other truths that go along with this. We must each have faith that we will be able to handle any situations or drawbacks that appear before us. This is part of our spiritual path and our personal soul growth which also contributes to the soul growth of all. Practicing this brings us closer to the unconditional loving energy of our God Force.

The key to your own spiritual practice is coming to a knowing and an understanding of what your life purpose is during this current incarnation. Maybe your soul needed to experience being homeless or losing your wealth. Or maybe you needed to experience grief for a loved one who has crossed over? Like me, maybe you needed the experience of a lifetime in which you did not have the gift of being a biological parent. For me too was the gut-wrenching grief of losing my mom, who was also my mentor and best friend.

One vital area that *The Secret* leaves out is the Universal Truth that as each of us advances further toward enlightenment and a vibrational energetic level closer to the God Source, our challenges sometimes become greater. Maybe one individual has chosen a life of fame and wealth. And let's say that during this chosen life of fame and wealth, the soul has other areas of work to attend to. And for some, their life purpose is holding space and the energy of proper frequency for others.

As I've previously explained, everything in our Universe consists of an energy, vibrational frequencies that can be measured. Once we learn to tap into this Universal Intelligence, we become part of what I like to refer to as Limitless Information for Everyone, or L.I.F.E. One of the "clair" words used to describe the ability of certain kinds of psychics is Claircognizance. Claircognizance is a clear knowing without any understanding of *how* you know the information. My Spirit Team has taught me that Claircognizance is actually the ability to tap into the Collective

Consciousness (Collective Intelligence). This is the realm of shared knowledge. My Team has shown it to me as being sort of like a databank or hard drive of information stored in the ethers. It's not actually stored in the ethers, however; they have shown it to me this way so that   my third-dimensional human brain can try to conceptualize this information. When you stop and think about it, this makes perfect sense! When someone claircognizantly *knows* information about a subject, yet has not *consciously* learned it in this lifetime, the Collective Intelligence *would* be the "place" this information comes from! How exciting is this concept my Spirit Team has shown me? This is yet another reason to study and learn psychic development with a qualified instructor. The more you learn to harness your personal psychic gifts, the easier it will be for you to tap into the Collective Intelligence. How awesome to have a wealth of knowledge at your fingertips anytime you need access to it! Channeling is yet another way that information not previously known can come through an individual. The channel connects to a higher being or consciousness and receives information that he or she had no way of knowing prior to the channeling session.

I have channeled an entity called Ashtar, of the Ashtar Command. The first time I met Ashtar, he came to me in the middle of the night and introduced himself. I had never heard of him prior to that evening. He telepathically said to me, "I am Ashtar of the Ashtar Command and I would like to work with you." I was so startled that I jumped out of bed and googled Ashtar Command. There it was as plain as day from others who had channeled him! People seem to get a kick out of the fact that psychics and mediums still get awed! If you have read my first book, *Mississippi Medium: My Journey from Southern Baptist to Talking to the Dead*, you may recall some of my out-of-this-world experiences. Yet, I still have those jaw-dropping moments of *wow, did this really just happen*?! Personally, I can't imagine living a so-called normal mundane life when we have such magic at our fingertips to uncover every day!

Ashtar is part of a consciousness called The Collective, that has volunteered to help those of us residing in the third dimension to awaken and ascend. Ashtar and his Galactic Team are also assisting us in breaking free from the matrix. Human beings have found themselves embedded in a control dynamic limited further by the Internet and social media. These higher-dimensional beings are channeling information through me and others to help us break these barriers and free ourselves from the matrix of domination. Primarily in recent history, the matrix of domination is mainly experienced by women and African Americans. When Ashtar channeled this term to me, the energy surrounding it was shown to be that of domination by those individuals vibrating at such a low frequency that we consider them to be evil. Their agenda is control through manipulation. Manipulation of our money supply, our media, and by pitting us against each other. Their maneuver of encouraging us to "choose sides" causes further division and alienation. And the further separated we think we are, the further we are from awareness of our true state of unity. Until the majority of humans can see that they are voluntarily participating in this system, true ascension of the collective cannot reach the fifth dimension. Part of the lesson in this lies in transcending this pattern and breaking free of the limiting beliefs that make up this reality.

How can we transcend these thought and belief patterns? There are many ways to accomplish this. One way is by tuning into the wisdom of your heart. It is my personal belief that our hearts harbor greater Universal Intelligence than our brains do. And scientific research supports this. HeartMath has been one of the premier research institutions studying the heart and brain connection. Rollin McCraty, Ph.D., one of HeartMath's original founders, said, "The biggest hidden source of stress on the planet is the disorganization of heart/mind, causing lack of resonance. Lack of alignment eats the life force and happiness out of humanity." McCraty also claims that the heart has access to information outside the boundaries of time and space.

How do we learn to listen to the intelligence or intuition of the heart? By going within. By unplugging from the mass media continually feeding us traumas and lower-vibrational words and images. By meditating, communing with nature, and learning to tune into our hearts. One thing I teach my psychic and mediumship students is to always make sure they are delivering messages to their clients from their heart chakra, always making sure the personal messages to themselves and others are from their heart space. The limiting human ego stemming from the brain's knowledge base is largely bypassed.

Grasping the exciting fact that we are indeed co-creators of our Universe is yet another way to transcend our limiting and separative beliefs. What do I mean by co-creators? Our Creator has given us free will. If we can break the limiting mindset that fate and destiny are set in stone and the details of our lives have already been molded, true freedom can occur. Imagine a world where we can wake up each day and write a new script for our lives! That world is here right in front of us! This is the gloriously liberating truth of what it means to co-create our reality.

A stunning visualization my Spirit Team has shown me is of starting each day in quiet contemplation, allowing guidance to come in, not only from our personal Spirit Team and Guides, but from the Collective Wisdom. The more we tap into this collective, the more freedom we will feel to co-create without boundaries. We as humans are only using a tiny portion of our potential.

Some of you may feel I am contradicting myself with the information included in chapter 5 regarding soul contracts. It is my belief that we do agree to certain soul contracts before we incarnate. This is our soul's way of experiencing opportunities for growth and evolution. Yet, with free will, we have the ability to set in motion the way our life is experienced as it unfolds. The difference is this: In the past, we have been taught that we can manifest anything our hearts desire. The *new* key is this: Before we set the intention of our manifestation, our consciousness needs to shift. If we are manifesting from our 3D perspective, our human ego will certainly get in the way. However, if we learn to release our human control and manifest from a higher vibration, this actually helps us release the limitations our human brain automatically puts on us.

When we are in a quiet space of meditation, we are already tapping into a higher-vibrational frequency. This is the place for manifestation magic to occur!

Another asset we humans have at our disposal is the Star Children who have incarnated. Star Children are human children born to help us heal our planet and ascend to higher vibrations. Many books have been written about Star Children; you may even be a Star Child yourself. Some of the common names given for such children are indigo, crystal, rainbow, and diamond. Star Children either arrive as a soul from a higher-vibrational frequency or a planet that vibrates at a higher frequency than our own. They are born already knowing we are all connected. Star Children have a special affinity for animals, plants, and all of nature. They tend to be quite sensitive and are often misunderstood.

Lee Carroll who channels Kryon first channeled information about Star Children in the 1970s. Since then, there has been much more information given regarding these souls. Many people believe that these children are a human/alien hybrid. It is my personal belief that the vast majority of highly psychic individuals have had contact with aliens and so-called UFOs. I realize that for many people, this concept may seem far-fetched. As I have always said, I must share my personal experiences from a place of honesty and truth. And my truth is that I am a Star Seed who has experienced visitation from aliens or extraterrestrials my entire life. Therefore, the information channeled by Lee Carroll and others has a huge resonance of truth for me.

There are several ways you can differentiate the various breeds of Star Seeds. Mainly the difference can be seen by certain gifted psychics in the color of the aura. Most Indigo Children have a predominantly blue color in their auric field. Crystal Children have a clearer or quartz-colored aura, and Rainbow Children have an aura consisting of a prism of several colors at one time. They also have very different and distinct personalities.

Several years ago, sometime around 2014, in meditation with the amazing spiritual teacher Lucy Finch of Altered Elements in Naples, Florida, I experienced a profound revelation. I was told that one of my soul contracts was to channel and write a book about the new children arriving. My human ego argued with my Spirit Team that I had not even had biological children in this lifetime, and how was I supposed to channel a book about children? I was told: This is part of your mission, and as an Indigo Star Seed yourself, you have the tools to comprehend and dissect the information channeled to you. During that meditation, I was told that the new children arriving would be named The Children of the Golden Ray and would be seen by those who can see auras as having a golden aura. I asked if any of these children had incarnated and I was told no. Since that time, I have been shown that the Golden Ray Children began incarnating in 2017. They are arriving from the twelfth dimension of consciousness. I am over the moon excited to channel the information on these children and write a book about them!

I have already had the pleasure of connecting with several parents of Golden Ray Children. The first one was when I was doing a reading for a couple in Asheville, North Carolina, and they asked me to tune into their young daughter and provide any information I could to help them parent her. As I tuned into her frequency, I immediately recognized the golden aura that I had been shown several years back. The purity of her auric field was awe-inspiring. As tears streamed down my face, I relayed the information to this couple that they were parents to a daughter from a new breed of Star Children called The Golden Rays. They were both quite emotional yet felt the sincerity of validation as they had always known she was very different. The second one was a child still in utero. As I was channeling information from one of my client's spirit guides, I was told that the child she was close to birthing into the world was a Golden Ray Child. I sat in awe as I connected with this divine being. My client admitted that she had experienced a deep knowing that this child was different. I explained how important it was for her as this gifted child's mother to make sure she aligned her own intuition and frequency, so she was equipped to parent this child in the highest good for all. This Golden Ray Mom registered for mine and Duann's Intuitive Development Classes right away.

Making the shift from a third-dimensional consciousness to a fifth-dimensional consciousness requires knowledge of certain steps. I enjoy seeing this as a type of bridge to another level of awareness. As we progress through our lives and begin to expand our individual awareness to include greater possibilities never before imagined, we begin to receive glimpses of this cosmic bridge. As we do our own inner work, all the while healing and growing, we draw closer to this bridge e so that we not only see it, but also grasp certain understandings about it. Part of this knowing is that once we make the decision to step onto this bridge and begin walking, we can never turn back. The thing is, once you step into the awe-inspiring magical energy of the bridge, you don't *want* to go back! You truly understand that the old world you left behind on the other side of that bridge is mundane and limiting. The energy of the old world feels confining and contracted. By contrast, the fifth dimension holds an expansive frequency. Simply walking on the bridge brings you an excitement you never dreamed possible. Effortlessly and instantly, you feel the oneness of the fifth dimension. Standing on this cosmic bridge, you witness and participate in the miracles unfolding in the beauty that surrounds you.

Part of the challenge of these times is navigating the world from the third dimension to the fifth. Many of us have done our best to keep one foot on either side of this bridge for many years now. Those of you who have experienced this understand it's not the easiest of tasks! And the longer you choose to linger on the fifth-dimensional side of the bridge, the more complicated it becomes to reside at all on the 3D side. In fact, it becomes almost impossible. It's important to acknowledge the fact that your physical body can't remain in the old energy, but also important not to judge those who have chosen to stay on the 3D side. We each have free will and can make these choices. I invite those of you who have yet to experience this awesome   energy to begin your journey to the bridge. I promise you: Your life will be forever enriched.

In 2009, my friend and colleague Sally Rice and I both received the same message from our Spirit Team. We were told that there would come a time in the future when there would be no more gray areas. At that time, souls would make a conscious choice of where they were going to reside. Which side of the bridge, if you will. That time is now. Now that we have entered the new decade of the 2020s, a choice must be made. As our Mother Earth raises her own vibrational frequency, it is becoming increasingly difficult for those who have chosen to remain in the unity energy of the fifth dimension to be in the energy of those who have consciously chosen to remain in the ego-dense energy of the divisive third dimension.

In closing this chapter, I would like to present this concept in a nice tidy package with a pretty bow on top! We are all interconnected by an etheric silver cord leading to the Infinite Source of all, our Creator God force. The essence of our Creator is true unconditional love for all, and the higher we can raise our personal vibrational frequency, the greater our experience of a love without condition or limitation. Given that we are truly interconnected -- woven together like threads in a design of ever-changing fabric -- I think it reasonable to assume that as we raise our personal vibration, and set the intention to help raise the vibration of others from a place of love and oneness, we all benefit.

The Secret did an outstanding job of introducing us to the concept of the Law of Attraction. Yet, in some instances, readers distorted the teachings to accommodate an extreme of greed, thereby stepping further into the energy of "me, myself, and I." In the fourteen years since this best-selling book was published, humanity has raised its collective vibrational frequency. It is now time to shift our mindset and consciousness to an energy of "we." The *Secret of the Secret* is so simple, yet one must achieve a certain level of awareness and energy vibration to truly comprehend how to set the wheels in motion. If you are reading this book, more than likely this shift has already occurred in your conscious awareness.

We are living in extraordinary times. It is a beautiful honor to have incarnated during these momentous shifts in evolution and consciousness. Each day, we are offered the gift of co-creating an exciting, magnificent Universe where all benefit in some way. This is what is needed to bring in the Age of Peace and Enlightenment.

Invitation to Explore:

I urge you to create an individual practice in which you begin each day in quiet contemplation. Set the intention that you are now the co-creator of your reality and your world with no boundaries and no limitations.

As you become more adept at co-creating your Universe, you will begin to notice that as long as you have applied the other Spiritual Laws in this book and you embrace your connection with all others, your individual wants and needs will begin to dovetail with those of all of humanity. And within this shift, you will begin to tap into limitless abundance for all. What does this mean? It simply means that the mentality of lack and poverty will gradually fade away, and your desires for an abundant life for yourself will emerge from your co-creating a Universe wherein *everyone* is divinely blessed. Can you *feel* the difference in manifesting in this way versus sitting in silence, visualizing and affirming for all you're worth that snazzy Ferrari and cocktails on the deck of *your* mansion?

Journal about your experiences and watch the magic unfold!

Chapter 9
Painting Your Masterpiece
★★★

"Sometimes when we gaze at the canvas of our life, our painting

may not appear flawless. Yet with each exquisite stroke, a

beautiful masterpiece of divine perfection begins to emerge."

In this final chapter, I am going to weave together nine practical steps to achieve the best version of your masterpiece. Most of us will not realize enlightenment during this lifetime; however, the goal is to show up each day and be the best version of ourselves that we can be. If we remember that every moment of every day, we have choices, the making of God-informed choices will be uppermost in our mind. Our thoughts are choices. We can choose positive ones, or we can choose to engage in stinkin' thinkin'. The choice is ours. With awakening comes the realization that we are all beautiful works in progress. And the more we get to know who we are on a soul level, the more we can be honest with ourselves.

Along with the raw splendor of honesty comes the opportunity for forgiveness, forgiveness of ourselves and others. Forgiveness is not about excuses, nor is it about holding on to stagnant energy from sorrows of the past. It pains me when I have clients who cannot forgive someone from their past and move forward into the present. They have recorded a mini movie in their mind about how much they've been hurt and wronged, and they hit replay almost daily. Be honest and ask yourself if you have one of these recordings in your own psyche that you will gladly play for anyone who will listen. Receiving compassion from another person for the pains you have endured provides but a momentary lift to the energy field. Yet when the recording is over and the other person moves forward with their own life, we are forced to accept the energy of where this leaves us.

We each have the choice to edit or scrap our mini movies! Proudly put on your writer's cap and begin to articulate the *new* script of your life. Remind yourself to step into fifth-dimensional energy prior to picking up the pen or striking the keys. Release limitations as you create. And as you sit in the director's chair, invite your Spirit Guides to join you in navigating the exciting plot twists and turns along the way. Remember that your Guides are holding the original script that you agreed to prior to incarnating. The inspiring thing is this. With our God-given free will, we can meet with our Spirit Team and co-create fresh and innovative scenarios anytime we choose!

These are the nine steps that have helped me in painting my own masterpiece. As you adopt these steps, you will find it easier to create your own awe-inspiring canvas.

1. **Remove the Ego** – What is the definition of ego? According to Merriam-Webster, ego is the self, especially as contrasted with another self or the world. Ego is the Latin word for "I." As we strive to embrace the vibration of the fifth dimension, we must remember that the new frequency is about the "we" and not the "I." Everything in life is about balance and moderation. I am not suggesting that we should not have healthy self-esteem and sense of self-worth. However, it is my belief that our ego keeps us in a place of separation and not unity. As Eckhart Tolle writes in *A New Earth*, "Give up defining yourself – to yourself or to others… Whenever you interact with people, don't be there primarily as a function or a role, but as the field of conscious Presence. You can only lose something that you have, but you cannot lose something that you are." This is what I am referring to when I recommend that you lose the more selfish aspects of ego. When we truly

grasp the fact that we are souls having an experience in a human body, the ego becomes much less of a factor. Our ego is involved in judgment, as well as our rational, critical thinking processes. According primacy to our ego prevents us from transcending old outdated thought processes. The sweet spot is getting to know the awareness behind the physical and material aspects of who we are and the role we play in this world. And by leaving the ego behind, we discover our true identity.

2. **Calm the Mind** - It is not possible to remain open and balanced and properly connected to Source Energy without devoting time to quiet the mind. This idea seems so simple, yet lack of time is one of the most common excuses I hear from my clients and others. *I can't quiet my mind,* some say. *My mind never stops working,* is the mantra of others. My response is this:" Then you need meditation even more!" In my opinion, everyone should also be practicing some form of yoga. Yoga provides a space for retreat from our busy daily lives. When we show up and step onto our mat, we begin to train our minds how to be present and in the moment. This is referred to as mindfulness. Mindfulness is learning to focus attention on what you are experiencing in the present moment without

judging yourself. Practicing yoga has been shown to increase mindfulness not only while we are in the class, but in every aspect of our lives. When we are living in the now, in the present moment, we are more easily able to let go of the past and stop fretting about the future.

3. **Practice Detachment** – We have become a society that places a great deal of value on material possessions. Many people define who they are as a person based on the size of their house, or how many homes they own, the brand of their watches, the designer label on their clothes, etc. I am certainly not suggesting that we should not desire nice things or luxurious items. Luxury is...well...luxurious! What I am referring to is the energy behind the possessions. I am inviting you to examine the *why* around your possessions and to be honest with yourself about whether you desire something because it provides you some level of comfort or joy, or whether you hold on to it to make a *statement* to other people. For example, there was a time in my life when I had a goal to own a Rolex. At the place I was in my life, this was one way I put a price tag on my level of success. The Law of Attraction worked for me and I purchased a watch that cost me over

$5,000. Looking back and being candidly honest with myself, I can see that wearing the watch made me *feel* more successful. Yet, in the grand scheme of things, that watch had absolutely nothing to do with the success I had attained! And then, as life often does in providing us growth opportunities, I found myself in a place where I needed to sell the watch in order to pay for necessities. At first, I was heartbroken. I told myself that I had worked so hard for that watch and I would certainly miss wearing it. In my moments of despair and feeling sorry for myself, my energetic vibration was certainly lowered. Yet, through detachment from this material item, I was given an opportunity to honestly examine the *why* of the watch I had chosen. Did the watch tell better time than my Timex or other watches had? No, it did not! When I sat with complete honesty with myself, it became apparent that I had wanted the watch so *others* would see and admire the level of my supposed success. At that time in my evolution, I placed greater value on what others thought of me than on who I knew myself to be. A similar story from my friend and colleague psychic medium Sally Rice brings a smile to my face. Sally had attained a great amount of material wealth throughout her life. One of her prized possessions was a Prada purse. During her spiritual evolution and consciousness expansion, her Spirit Guides softly suggested that she release the attachment to her Prada purse. Sally argued and pouted as we humans tend to do, and said out loud, "But I love my Prada purse!" And then she decided to conduct a little experiment with the Universe. Sally declared, "OK, Universe! I will drop off my Prada at a nonprofit, and I will release my attachment to this purse, but in return, I want some sort of acknowledgement that my deed has been noticed." Sally was attempting to practice her own version of the Law of Attraction while also expanding her level of consciousness. After dropping off her beloved Prada purse and stepping into the energy of complete detachment, she drove to a healthy grocery store to pick up a few items. As she was walking inside, a nice young man walked up to her and said, "Hi, I have a gift for you." Sally, never one to turn down a sincere gift, followed him back out to the parking lot and he opened the back of his van. "My wife hand-sews beautiful purses and my Spirit Guides just told me to give one of them to you." He continued, "I'm not sure why I'm supposed to gift you with one, but I have learned to listen to my Team, so please take the purse and enjoy it." Sally marveled at the magic that had just unfolded right before her eyes and thanked the Universe for the proof she had requested. This event still makes me tear up. We truly do live in a magical place of abundance. I invite you to examine some of the material possessions you have acquired. Be honest with yourself. Do you have these possessions because they bring you joy or comfort, or do you have them to impress others? Again, there is absolutely nothing wrong with luxury and comfort! Luxuries are among the gifts showered upon us by this amazing planet we call home. The lesson lies in detaching from the place of ego.

4. **Spiritual Mentors and Teachers** – I would not be where I am today without the lessons learned from my own spiritual teachers and mentors. It saddens me when I hear people say, "I don't need classes or knowledge from others, because I was born with my wisdom and gifts." This is pure ego. We ALL have something to learn from others who have either experienced more life lessons or who have studied with others in order to share the knowledge they received. Semi-jokingly I say to my students, "With certain spiritual teachers, you learn how you *don't* want to be or how you *don't* want to do things!" Yet, you still learned something. This does not mean that you place all your questions and answers to life in the hands of someone else. It simply means that you are receptive to

the knowledge and insights of others, learning from them while honoring your individual guidance. You take what resonates with you from the wisdom of each teacher and kindly leave the rest behind. We should never stop learning and growing! Personally, I crave to learn from others who have more life experience than I do. This does not lessen my value as a spiritual teacher. In fact, it strengthens it. I still laugh when I recall something one of my spiritual teachers, John Holland, shared with our class. John showed his reverence and respect for one of his teachers, James Van Praagh, by making a joke. John chuckled as he told us students, "As I climb the ladder of my success, I am always looking up at the behind of James Van Praagh." He goes on to say, "And I'm OK with that! What an honor to be staring up at James's behind as I climb higher myself! James will always be a few rungs above me because he's had more experience in the world of mediumship." Show reverence and respect for your spiritual teachers. No matter how many years I have been serving the Spirit World, I have never lost respect for the teachers I have had along the way. It doesn't mean that I give my power away to them. It simply means I honor what they taught me and the ways they assisted me along my soul's path. You would do well to find a spiritual teacher whom you feel drawn to; then watch your life burst into colors and shapes you could never have imagined.

5. **Learn Vibrational Frequency** – Living a human experience gives us vast opportunities to learn from our mistakes. With practice and dedication, we can learn to stay in the habit of keeping our thoughts pure, our words uplifting, and our actions wholesome. Strive to be an inspiration to others. I urge you to always be on the lookout to help one another with this, as practice makes perfect. If you hear a friend or loved one speaking words that put themselves or another down, even in a joking manner, tell them to cancel-clear their words and speak them over again in a positive way. Get in the habit of bearing witness to your own words and the energy behind them. Have fun with this. Leave little love notes around the house that you will find with sayings such as "I am abundant," "I am healthy," "I am kind," "I am an inspiration to others," etc. Think about how your energy level will automatically shift when you come across these uplifting words. Another fun thing we can do to help shift other people's energy is to offer them kind words, such as genuine compliments and encouragement. Make a pact with yourself that you will choose at least one stranger a day whom you will compliment or cheer in some way. You

can offer compliments on what they are wearing or their beautiful eyes or smiles. Recently, I told a woman that she had a beautiful aura, and her grateful smile lit up the room. When we compliment someone, we in turn get an energy boost. Win-win and joy-joy for everyone!

6. **Engage in Life** – As discussed in chapter four, we are unable to manifest our heart's desires without understanding the Spiritual Law of Action. When we actively participate in our lives and take the necessary steps in the direction of something we desire, momentum is created which in turn helps to activate the Law of Vibration and brings more success with the Law of Attraction. For example, it takes more than a desire for someone to fulfill their ambition to be the greatest athlete of all time. Along with that desire comes dedication and actually putting the steps into motion to reach the desired result. First, the right coach or mentor must be located. After the trainer is found, certain hours of each day must be spent in training. The Law of Attraction will not work if the athlete simply sits there in lotus position, willing him or herself to be the greatest athlete of all time. I have told countless clients that the chance of their soulmate simply walking up to their front door one day and sweeping them off

their feet is highly unlikely. We must take action to get involved in activities that bring us joy and excitement, action that puts us in situations where we are likely to meet our soulmates. When we actively show up as excited participants in our lives, this sends the Universe an energy signature that we are doing our part to harness our hopes and dreams. Remaining fluid and adaptable helps a great deal in engaging in life. For instance, if we choose to live in the same box without ever stepping outside of it or being open to new experiences, a stuck and stagnant energy ensues. My recommendation is this: Don't simply climb outside your box. Make designs with your box. Mold it into various geometric shapes and see what excitement the Universe delivers to your doorstep then! And I promise you, if you're true to this task, the "box" the Universe delivers your gifts in will look like nothing you could have ever imagined! Always remember you are the co-creator of your Universe, so have fun with this.

7. **Release Your Fears** – Facing one's fears is not for the faint of heart. However, since we know that everything is energy and everything we think, feel, and do comprises an energy, we must come to terms with the fact that our fears are holding us back. Fear is a low-vibrational energy. Fear is a lack of trust. With his usual

humor, Mark Twain said, "I have been through some terrible things in my life, some of which actually happened." When I feel myself slipping into the energy of fear, I ask myself, "What is the worst that can happen?" It's important not to sweep our fears under the proverbial rug, because fear is a legitimate human emotion. Yet if we can learn to shift our fears into courage and compassion, just imagine the sublime results we will witness. I simply adore this quote from Marianne Williamson: "Our deepest fear is not that we are inadequate. Our deepest fear is that we are powerful beyond measure. It is our light, not our darkness, that most frightens us. We ask ourselves, 'Who am I to be brilliant, gorgeous, talented, fabulous?' Actually, who are you not to be? You are a child of God." In order to manifest the divine masterpiece that you were meant to create, you must release your fears. This does not mean we scold ourselves for our fears. What it means is that we lovingly learn to turn our fears into courage. We simply cannot walk a spiritual path burdened by our fears. This is not something that happens overnight, however. There are legitimate fears that arise in the course of changing and evolving. At times, there will be things and people who leave our lives as we expand beyond their comfort zones. Honor the grief of the loss while bravely recognizing that someone leaving our lives creates space for others to step in. And congratulate yourself for the fears you have transcended on the liberating wings of courage.

8. **Trust and Surrender** – As discussed in chapter 4, the Spiritual Law of Faith plays a major role in manifesting our masterpieces. The word surrender sounds so sexy and sultry and easy, yet it is one of the most challenging states for humans to realize. We feel powerful when we are in control. It gives us a false sense of comfort and security. Yet that's just it. Ultimately, is a *false* sense of protection. In my humble view of spiritual evolution, we must learn to trust not only ourselves, but also our Creator and Spirit Team. It's imperative that we discern the difference between trusting ourselves when we are in perfect alignment with our Higher Selves and trusting ourselves when we are behaving foolishly, without regard for ourselves and others.

9. **Unconditional Love and Oneness** – If I needed to choose just one word to represent the energy of the fifth dimension, it would certainly be oneness. It is nearly impossible to experience oneness in the third dimension. Oneness extends beyond the five senses,

beyond the ordinary reality. Have you ever had a moment of feeling pure bliss, and the ecstasy was so sublime that you had a moment of feeling at one with All That Is, and more? These are fleeting glimpses of what awaits us in the higher dimensions. My Guides have shown me that as we move into 2020 and beyond, our attention needs to be focused on loving ourselves first. If we can't truly love ourselves without conditions, it is not possible for us to genuinely love another. And by fully loving every aspect of ourselves, we are reminded that we are indeed One. I invite you to practice standing in front of the mirror each morning and, gazing deeply into your eyes to the depths of your soul, say, "I love you." This is powerful medicine, my friends.

It has been my honor to accompany you on this journey with me. By raising the curtain on previously private scenes of my personal heartbreak and grief and making my best effort to share the discoveries I've made along the way, I sincerely hope you have received additional inspiration. "Powerful beyond measure," you are now equipped to paint your own divine masterpiece in ways that excite and delight you.

Finally, I would like to extend accolades to Rhonda Byrne for introducing us to *The Secret* fourteen years ago. It is my belief that the concepts in her best-selling book went a long way toward waking people up to their unlimited worthiness and infinite potential. My hope is that by reading my book, you have received some profound and enlightening secrets that will further assist you on your life's amazing journey.

The Light in me sees and honors the Light in each of you.

Namaste.

Epilogue

★★★

To Mandy's delight, the small town of Fairhope, Alabama, proved to be majestically beautiful. And the people were so friendly and welcoming. *I guess there is truth to what is said about Southern hospitality,* Mandy found herself thinking. Fairhope was close enough to her job in Mobile to make her commute fairly effortless. She and Teddy had settled into a small cottage within walking distance to the cute downtown area. While she liked her job and the people who worked there, Mandy knew in her heart of hearts that there was more she wanted to accomplish in her life.

Mandy spent her free time enjoying yoga and meditation, which had helped her reach a deeper place of contemplation. She was reading books on spirituality and ascension which were really helping her understand the deeper meanings of life and the Universe. However, she was still flustered and frustrated over her perceived manifestation failures over the past year. Nevertheless, Mandy knew how important it was to stay positive and pay attention to her thoughts and emotions. As she woke to the dawn of each new day, she reminded herself to practice gratitude for her courage and how far she had come. She felt peaceful and more in alignment than she ever had before. Mandy yearned for companionship, yet she had detached from putting constraints on what this actually looked like or how it would manifest for her. And she certainly recognized that she had been settling and trying to fit a square peg into a round hole in her years spent with John. Over time, she had forgiven him and even performed a healing cord-cutting ceremony at an event she had attended the month prior. She was finally at peace with his infidelity and the choices he had made, recognizing that negative thoughts of him took up precious real estate in the recesses of her mind.

One beautiful June day, Mandy decided to walk to her favorite coffee shop. She had grown to love and adore the small town of Fairhope and finally felt at home living there. There were times, however, in her daydreams, that the Florida beaches would seem to call out her name, their waves whispering sweet nothings in her ear. And when she really allowed herself to reflect on what she would want to be remembered for, the animals and their welfare always came to mind. But for now, at this juncture in her life, she considered herself happy and content.

"Your regular caramel latte with coconut milk, Mandy?" Paige smiled as Mandy entered the café. "Sounds heavenly," Mandy said as she settled into a comfy chair by the large bay window.

They exchanged pleasantries and Paige told Mandy another hilarious story about her new rescue dog, Lucky. As Mandy took a sip of her latte, she noticed a handsome man walk into the shop. As their eyes met, she felt – although she knew it was perhaps a corny allusion – that her world had stopped turning. After he grabbed a coffee, he walked over to Mandy and introduced himself. "Hi, I'm Alex," he smiled, holding out his hand in greeting. Mandy tried to gather her composure as she introduced herself, but felt as if she would disappear into the depths of his green eyes and not be able to come back out! "Do you mind if I join you? I'm just here visiting for a few days. I live in Pensacola, where I run an animal rescue nonprofit and I needed a break!" He continued, "As you can imagine, it's a lot of work, but a passion that I care a great deal about."

Mandy noted to herself that the sensation she was experiencing reminded her of the strange feeling she'd in Ms. Thelma's presence. There was a calm yet electric sensation in the pit of her stomach. Two hours went by as Mandy and Alex effortlessly chatted as if they had known each other forever. In truth, they both felt they had been reunited with someone who was monumental in their lives. Alex invited Mandy to dinner that night, and over dessert she recounted her lifelong dream of rescuing animals. Mandy felt a sense of safety with Alex that she had never felt before. Every time she gazed into his kind eyes, she had a sense that he knew her to the depths of her soul. They spent every moment together over the next few days and, as Alex prepared his return to Florida, he admitted to Mandy that he had never truly believed in love at first sight until now. He explained that he was secure in where he was in his life and had not really dated since his divorce several years back, but after meeting her, he could not possibly imagine a life without her in it. Mandy told Alex she felt the same way.

As fate would have it, their commute to see each other was only a one-hour drive. They continued dating and getting to know each other over the next eight months and on Valentine's Day, Alex got down on his knee and proposed. Later that night, Mandy was reminded that the proposal was exactly as she had envisioned several years back. The only difference was the person down on one knee. *Wow, this is interesting!* Mandy reflected. *Maybe the Law of Attraction does work.* However, there were other factors at play, not yet known. Alex and Mandy planned a June wedding on the shores of Fairhope, Alabama, 12 months to the day from when they had met. Mandy was further delighted when she found the perfect wedding dress that looked just like one she had cut out of the magazine years before. When Alex took Mandy's hand in his to proudly say his vows, tears were streaming down both of their faces.

Mandy's coworkers were sad to see her leave, but over-the-moon happy at the love she had found. Several months after moving to Florida and going to work with Alex at his animal rescue foundation, Mandy received yet another surprise. Alex came home filled with childlike excitement as he told her to get in the car with him. "We are going on a little adventure!" Alex said, his eyes dancing with enthusiasm. As they pulled up to the house Alex had discovered for them, Mandy shook her head in disbelief. The house looked exactly like the one she had cut out from the magazine while she was living in Michigan. *How could this be?* she wondered. Alex twirled Mandy around as she kissed him all over his face. "I love it," she declared.

They settled in and made the house their home. Mandy's favorite part of the house was the large fenced-in yard which gave their many rescue dogs plenty of room to play. Of course, the dogs lived inside with them as part of their family, but Shanti, their massive Lab and shepherd mix, adored running as fast as she could around the expansive yard, chasing the less than thrilled border collie.

A few months later, Mandy's friend Denise mailed her a copy of a book she had just read and loved. Mandy sat down and devoured the pages of *Secrets of the Secret* in a few short days. Her mind was reeling as the words on each page finally brought answers to her questions as to why she had previously been unsuccessful at using the Law of Attraction to manifest. Mandy smiled as she realized that she *had* been successful at manifesting everything she had wanted. It just took various twists and turns and had different timing than what she had in mind. The fact that she was living on the beaches of Florida with her soulmate while helping him run an animal rescue still sent shockwaves of delight down her spine. "What are the odds?" Mandy asked Teddy, curled up by her side. Teddy gifted her with a sly gaze and smile, as he absolutely adored Alex. *All Mom had to do was ask me all those years ago and I would have told her how it was,* Teddy surmised in his innate kitty wisdom.

Later that night over dinner, Mandy shared with Alex all she had read in *Secrets of the Secret*. Alex commented, "I guess it would make sense that we have other Spiritual Laws at our fingertips to use along with the Law of Attraction. And one is not any more important than the others." Mandy smiled as she reflected on how she had put the Law of Faith in place when she trusted and surrendered and moved to Alabama. "I could have used my free will and chosen to ignore the signs and synchronicities and forced a move to Florida," she shared with her husband, "but it would not have been Pensacola, and I would probably not have met you."

As Mandy lay in bed that night holding Alex's hand, she marveled at how amazing life can be as long as we learn to get out of our own way. An inspiring vision wafted through her mind of herself teaching and leading workshops, coaching others in the use of all the Spiritual Laws to paint the masterpiece of their lives. *I will put the Law of Action into play and research the best places to lead the workshops, while also watching for signs and synchronicities to light my way.* She then offered up her prayers of gratitude, reminding herself of the words Ms. Thelma had said to her all those years ago about the riches of the Universe falling at her feet. "This magical, mystical Universe has certainly delivered riches in ways I never dreamt possible," Mandy whispered as she closed her eyes, excited for the dreams to come.

ABOUT THE AUTHOR

The Mississippi Medium, Jill M Jackson, is an international award winning highly sought after Psychic Medium and Spiritual Teacher having won such prestigious awards such as the 2016 and 2015 Psychic of the Year from Best American Psychics! She was also awarded the 2014 Social Activism Award from Best American Psychics for her volunteer work with animals.

One of her great passions is being of service as a Spiritual Teacher and helping others ignite, refine, and hone their gifts! Whether you are desiring to deepen your Intuition to help in your career and personal life or whether you feel you have a calling to become a Professional Psychic or Medium, consider allowing Jill to help you navigate your way! Visit **www.JillMJackson.com**.

Jill is the co-creator of Soul Synergy Center in Flowood, Mississippi. Soul Synergy Center is a metaphysical wellness center offering yoga, reiki, meditations, sound healing, metaphysical new age products, and Psychic and Mediumship readings.

Jill lives in Mississippi with her beloved husband Daniel and their four dogs.

Made in the USA
Columbia, SC
10 February 2020